JOURNEYS T[...]
BRIGAN[...]A

JOHN DIXON
AND
PHILLIP DIXON

VOLUME TWO:

Walks in Ribblesdale, Malhamdale & Central Wharfedale

JOURNEYS THROUGH BRIGANTIA
VOLUME TWO:
RIBBLESDALE, MALHAM & CENTRAL WHARFEDALE
By
John Dixon & Phillip Dixon

Copyright © John Dixon & Phillip Dixon 1990

Published by Aussteiger Publications,
8 Back Skipton Road, Barnoldswick BB8 5NE.
Tel. (0282) 812741

Typeset by:
Hargreaves Steel Limited,
133 Henry Street, Church, Accrington, Lancashire BB5 4EP

Printed by:
Lamberts of Settle

First edition, November 1990

ISBN 1 872764 02 9

The sketch maps in this book are intended to indicate the route in a general way. Walkers should use Ordnance Survey Pathfinder maps to locate exact routes.

Whilst all the walks use established and definitive footpaths, walkers are requested to respect the privacy of residents and not to stray from the footpaths.

Please observe the Country Code.

Dedicated to David Hazell who first gave me the idea of writing Historic Walking Guides. Thanks, Ginger — John

AUSSTEIGER PUBLICATIONS

Contents

JOURNEYS THROUGH BRIGANTIA

VOLUME ONE:
Craven, Airedale & Wharfedale

VOLUME TWO:
Ribblesdale, Malham & Central Wharfedale

VOLUME THREE:
Lower Wharfedale, Wasburndale & Ilkley Moor

VOLUME FOUR:
Upper Ribblesdale, The Three Peaks
& Upper Wharfedale

VOLUME FIVE:
Nidderdale, Knaresborough & Wensleydale

VOLUME SIX:
Swaledale, Teesdale & the Vale of Eden

VOLUME SEVEN:
The Lune Valley & Forest of Bowland

A Lakeland series will be entitled

JOURNEYS INTO RHEGED

INTRODUCTION

The books in this series are not intended for the 'plod-on-Larry' type of walker but for the more discerning and adroit wanderer who seeks a meaningful exploration of the Landscape, returning with a fuller appreciation of the environments they have ventured into.

The walks undertaken take on the nature of a journey through a bygone world, being the central areas of a once tribal zone known as Brigantia, for the most part centred on the Yorkshire Dales, an area of outstanding natural beauty and historical heritage.

We shall follow a Celtic peoples as they emerge in the dawn of Northern history to become the most famed of British tribes to resist the might of Rome, and their emergence from that period only to face further struggles from European incomers, the stories of which have come down to us in Arthurian legend.

Fortunately other sources exist for us to reconstruct those times: the disciplines of Archaeology, History, Philology and Architecture are brought together and presented here in a format that all can understand and gain from.

The walks themselves stand in their own right and take the reader-cum-explorer through the finest and most diverse countryside that can be found anywhere in Britain. Great care has been taken to check out all the walking instructions, and for this we thank the Saturday Historic Walkers who turn out every week in all weathers. Thank you all. — J. L. & P. G. Dixon.

Included in this book are some very fine drawings by the Trawden artist, Bob Mann. In future books, Bob's drawings will play an important role in illustrating the main features of the walks. He has previously worked with me on our book 'Historic Walks around the Pendle Way'. — J. D.

HISTORICAL BACKGROUND

At the time of the birth of Christ the Brigantian people held sway over a tract of territory which stretched from the Mersey and Humber to the Scottish Lowlands. Despite the importance of the Brigantian state very little field evidence of its people has survived in most parts of the North of England.

However, due to a chance interaction of geography and history, the upper Aire and Wharfe valleys are exceptionally rich in archaeology of the Brigantian Age.

The field systems, villages, farmsteads and chattels found at settlement sites allow the historian to reconstruct this Romano-British society. The settlement sites of Malhamdale and the surrounding areas represent the fringe of Brigantian economic activity. The heartlands of Brigantia were the coastal plains of Lancashire, the Solway plain, the Vale of York and the Pennine valleys of the Wharfe, Aire, Calder, Ribble, Lune, Tees, Tyne and Eden.

Unfortunately for the field archaeologist these are the very areas which have been subject to constant occupation and resettlement throughout the ages. This century has seen the destruction of a large part of the field archaeology of lowland areas of Britain because of new farming methods.

It is a strange society which encourages cereal farmers to plough out a historical site — so as to grow wheat which rots in intervention food mountains. However, if it was not for Community subsidy, most of our upland farmers would be forced from the land. This would mark the death of part of our northern landscape with commuters replacing people.

At the coming of Rome the lands north of the Humber were not strangers to the threat of invasion. The federation of tribes which made up Brigantia was probably formed to counter the twin threats of the Picts and Belgic Celts. The Picts lived north of the Clyde and Forth, a fierce non-Celtic people whose origins are lost in the distant past. The Belgic were a late wave of Celtic aristocracy from mainland Europe who established themselves in the South of England in the first century or so before the birth of Christ. The 'new aristocracy' established trade links with Gaul and Imperial Rome, introduced a cash economy and new methods of political and military power. In many tribes the Belgic aristocracy replaced the old aristocracy. This process seems to have had little impact on the Pennine and Welsh peoples. In east Yorkshire the Belgic kingdom of the Parisi was established, the most northern outpost of their culture.

This kingdom, based on the Yorkshire Wolds, had the North Sea and the Humber marshes as its hinterlands and a long open border with Brigantia — the state could have been established with Brigantian consent. On the other hand the Parisi could have established themselves on the Wolds before the Brigantian federation was formed. However the Parisi could have been given land on the Wolds by the Brigantian royal house, so as to boost the military and political power of the royal household.

The Roman threat was held at bay for over 25 years by a treaty by which Rome recognised Brigantia as an allied state — a marcher kingdom to secure the northern frontier of Rome in Britain. The southern kingdoms had been rapidly overrun by the Romans; many patriots took refuge in Brigantia and north Wales.

The patriarchal anti-Roman faction rallied around the Queen's consort Venutius and the matriarchal pro-Roman faction rallied to Queen Cartimandua. In AD 51 Cartimandua, in pursuance of her pro-Roman policy, handed over the British guerrilla leader Caractucus to the Romans, after he had sought asylum. This act of shame prompted a palace revolution and civil war between pro and anti Roman factions.

However, with Roman support, Cartimandua restored her power and continued to reign until Venutius' second revolt in AD 69. In this year Cartimandua divorced Venutius for his armour bearer Vellocatus — civil war broke out. The Romans rescued the Queen but left the anti-Roman party in power in Brigantia.

Instead of coming to terms with Venutius the Imperial leadership decided to invade and push the northern frontier of the province to the Solway and Tyne. In hindsight this policy was a major error of judgment — because the Pennine hinterland of Brigantia was never pacified.

The first stage of the conquest of Brigantia would have been the establishment of Chester and York as Legionary base camps. Advancing from Wroxeter the establishment of Chester divided the Pennine tribes from their allies in

North Wales. The Dee also provided a base for amphibious operations in the Irish Sea. The movement of the Ninth Legion from Lincoln to York was a more difficult advance, as it represented a thrust into the heartlands of Brigantia.

The most direct line of advance from Lincoln was a march directly north crossing the Humber at Brough, then following the crest of the Wolds to within a few miles of York. A secondary line of advance was a thrust along what is now the route of the Great North Road, east of the Pennines and west of the wetlands of the Humber basin. Once established York could be supplied and reinforced by water transport on the Ouse and Humber.

Despite the massive investment in manpower that the Stanwix Camp represents — it is unlikely that the army of Venutius which mobilised there in AD 70 fought a static war of defence. The Celts knew that Rome could be defeated — for had not Boudicca raised London and Colchester — and in the time of Augustus had not the Germans liberated themselves?

The struggle for Brigantia would have been fought out in the dense forests of the Vale of York. Having dispersed the Confederate army, Imperial forces would have pushed forward to the Tyne to establish a new northern frontier.

On the west side of the Pennines the line of advance would have followed a route determined by the lowest fording points on the Mersey, Ribble and Lune. To secure this route a parallel military road was driven from Manchester to Ribchester and on to the Lune Valley and northwards to the Vale of Eden. The Stonegate road between Newcastle and Carlisle was established along the new frontier.

To facilitate rapid troop movements between either side of the Pennines and to control these uplands four trans-Pennine military roads were established. The routes protected by auxiliary forts were between Manchester and York via Strandedge, Manchester to Ilkley via Blackstone Edge, through Craven between York and Ribchester and the high Stainmore route.

At the close of the 1st century AD a study of the deployment of the Imperial Legions of Rome illustrates the main external threats to the Empire. Three legions were stationed in Syria to counter the ever present Persian Empire. The Rhine and Danube borders were held by about a dozen legions each, North Africa had a single legion containing the Berber raiders. It is therefore surprising that the Province of Britain was garrisoned by three legions.

A legion consisted of about 5,000 heavy infantry and 150 horse. Besides the three legions based at Caerwent, Chester and York, the complex of frontier defences of Hadrian was manned by over 20,000 auxiliary troops. A further 20,000 troops were placed in the Pennine and Welsh forts. It can be concluded that in the territory of the Brigantian people, the Imperial authorities thought it necessary to provide a garrison of over 40,000 troops. Brigantia was probably the most militarised zone in the Roman Empire.

The Romans faced three, and in later years four, potential military threats in Brigantia. The main threat came from the Picts and Celt tribes who lived north of the wall. Irish and Pictish sea-borne raiders were a danger from the Solway to the Mersey. From the late third century Germanic pirates raided the east coast. The fourth problem came from within the Northern Provence — internal revolts of the Pennine tribesmen. The forts at Elslack, Ilkley and Bainbridge were occupied at intervals throughout the Roman period — this is clear evidence of the internal enemy the Imperial Authority faced in the Pennine Zone.

The key combat units of the Brigantian garrison were based at York and Chester, placed so as to be able to respond in a flexible manner to any crisis in or beyond the military zone. The first priority of the commander of the northern garrison was to ensure that incursions into the zone did not take place; failing this incursions were to be neutralised within the zone. The zone existed to provide defence in depth for the rich arable parts of the Province south of the Trent. The peace and authority of the 'Pax Romana' in Britain was built on the success of the military zone. What is remarkable is that the inhabitants of the military zone seem to have been able to maintain a spirit of resistance throughout the Imperial period.

Roman authority in Craven was maintained by the two garrison forts of Elslack and Ilkley which controlled either side of the Aire Gap. Ilkley was built around AD 80, evacuated under Hadrian, re-occupied in the mid second century and destroyed in the uprising of 197. The fort was rebuilt in stone under Severius and then occupied to the end of the fourth century. The limited excavations at Elslack between 1919 and 1921 point to a similar pattern of occupation. The status of the Roman fort at Long Preston is long overdue re-investigation — but it clearly did not have the same long period of occupation as Elslack and Ilkley. I would suggest that Long Preston and the marching camp on Malham Moor probably date from the initial invasion of Brigantia. To the west of Craven a powerful fort existed at Ribchester, and to the north deep in the heart of the Dales at Bainbridge a succession of stone forts were occupied from the time of Agricola to the end of the fourth century. Further afield the Stainmore route was protected by forts at Bowes and Greta Bridge.

In terms of political and military power the system of military roads was of greater importance than the auxiliary forts. The road system was used by the army for rapid troop movements, by the Imperial postal service, civilian officials and local farmers marketing their produce. The greater part of the native population lived in Wharfedale and Ribblesdale, and would have been in everyday contact with the garrisons at Ilkley and Elslack. The Imperial post and patrols would pass along the roads on a daily basis. However the evidence put forward in this book suggests that the overall impact of the 'Pax Romana' was little more than a military occupation — with little impact on the native society.

Individual patterns of land ownership, organisation and farming methods were not disturbed in Roman Brigantia. The estates of the Royal House and chief warriors would have been seized for the Imperial domain, though most local landlords would have retained their estates. There are many documented examples of Roman officials extorting land from provincials, but these are exceptions rather than the rule. Like the British Empire in India, a new ruling caste superimposed itself on the existing system — the new built upon the old.

The geographical conditions in the Pennines dictated that the Brigantian people followed a largely pastoral way of life. In the non-limestone parts of Craven the typical settlement was the ringed earthwork. This type of earthwork in encountered on the first two walks in this Volume: at Steeling Hill a three-quarter acre settlement site is enclosed by a low earthwork, nearby Swinden Camp encloses 1½ acres and in the second walk the Park House enclosure covers two-thirds of an acre.

These low earthworks are all that remains of a ditch, vallum and palisade. The purpose of this barrier was to protect the settlement and its stock from wild beasts and casual theft. Inside of these enclosures would have stood round huts and stock pens. Over 10,000 Iron Age enclosures of this type have been recorded in Ireland, but in the Pennine regions where such enclosures are also common there is a desperate need for these sites to be recorded for posterity.

On the limestone uplands we again find enclosures, but in this area stone walls replaced the earthbanks and palisade. On Walk 4 we discover a site made up of several enclosures and dwellings at the Horseshoe settlement above

Settle. Comparable settlements are found on Walk 5 at Stridebut Edge and Langscar, and Grassington on Walk 6. Walk 9 is particularly rich in limestone settlements including at Cow Close a rectangular Iron Age dwelling — a primitive prototype of the mediaeval long house which evolved into the barn/house Pennine type of dwelling.

Outside the enclosure lay a complex field system — small arable plots to supply the community with cereals, probably a Rye-like grain grown on an infield-outfield system. The infield was kept fertile by a rich dressing of manure provided by the outfield herds. Crops of primitive grains may have been supplemented by pulses and hay for winter fodder.

Household goods can be divided into two groups of finds, the domain of the womenfolk and the men. Each household required a saddle quern, tests have shown that these querns were not a very effective way of grinding corn. It would have required many hours of laborious effort to produce the flour for a household. Cooking took place on an open fire, the unleavened bread baked on hot stones. The diet of Rye bread would be supplemented by dairy products, wild fruits and the occasional feast of meat.

Textiles were made on a primitive loom with thread spun using a horn comb, drawing spoon and spindle — see Victoria settlement Walk 4. A woman's day would have been dominated by child rearing, grinding corn, cooking and attending livestock. The production of textiles would have been a seasonal occupation following the spring shearing. It is not possible to determine if men were involved in the production of textiles.

The evidence of the men of a household is mainly drawn from metallic objects — axes, knives and spears being the tools of the herdsman and warrior alike. Each community would have required a wooden push plough to turn the sod, and an oven of sorts would have been essential to dry grain for storage. Personal possessions would have been few but treasured.

The basic kilt cum cloak of the Brigantian required a device to hold it together at the shoulder with a brooch or the like. A fine example of such a brooch was found at Attermire Cave — the brooch dated from the third or fourth century A.D. (Walk 4). Ale would have been brewed and stored in an earthenware pot and drunk from a horn vessel. Each household would have had bone combs, fish hooks and needles.

As can be seen from this evidence a fairly detailed picture of life in upland

Brigantia can be envisaged. These insights have to be balanced by our lack of knowledge. The Brigantian uplander lived in an isolated enclosure settlement or a small cluster of such settlements — but was this typical of upland areas only? If we consider matters of dress did the Brigantian go barefoot like the mediaeval Irish or Scottish highlander — or did he have a primitive sort of boot like the southern Celts.

At Attermire Cave a dismantled chariot and other goods belonging to a nobleman were hidden and never recovered. Under what circumstances were these goods deposited? — does this reflect social unrest, invasion or revolt against Rome? The discovery of abandoned Roman lead pigs supports the theory of unrest and revolt. Returning to the chariot, what was its purpose, does this show that a native family made use of the Roman road system or was it purely for ceremonial use?

At Aldborough, many Roman or native nobles built fine town houses at the seat of local government for the Brigantian state. On the eastern flank of the Pennines some native landlords established villas, but with the exception of Kirk Sink, Gargrave (Vol.1), this trend towards Romanisation did not spread to the central or western Pennines.

The most difficult subject to consider is that of belief. We know that the Brigantian religion was dominated by the cult of the severed head. The heads of dead heroes decorated holy shrines, some heads carved from the living rock and some hacked off the corpses on the battlefield. The Roman Annals inform us that the druidic caste had a stronghold in North Wales, archaeological evidence from a Cheshire peat bog confirms human ritual murder.

In this volume we find cave burials on Walk 4 and a Celtic stone head on Walk 1. At Seaty Hill tumulus the Brigantes had no objection to re-using a Bronze Age site to bury their dead. No evidence however has come to light to support the theory of human sacrifice being practised in the Pennine area.

Both the Roman and the Celtic pantheon was crowded. A modest spring could have its own diety, as could a river, family, clan or tribe. At Ilkley a Roman set up an altar to a local Celtic water (Sulus) diety. The religion of Roman and Celt was based on ritual and sacrifice but gave no guide to the regulation of the affairs of men. There is little evidence that the Brigantian society adopted anything of substance from the Imperial Culture. The Romans on the other hand fervently added the Celtic gods to their own Pantheon adopting Brigantia as the provincial diety.

The Brigantian Pennine people continued to follow a life dominated by seasonal flock movements, subject to but independent from Roman authority. This is not surprising for what did Imperial Rome have to offer these semi-nomadic people? It is therefore surprising that Rome did give the Brigantian people one revolutionary innovation.

Christianity arrived in Britain as a subversive eastern cult in the 2nd century. By the 3rd century the cult was well established in the towns of Roman Britain. However, at the close of the 4th, it had not established itself as a major faith within the province. In the south of England the 5th century saw Christianity swept aside by Germanic paganism.

A different scenario presents itself in the north of England. There is evidence of a Christian community at the western end of Hadrian's Wall in the final decades of Roman power. At this time the northern garrison was a polyglot force of local levies backing up mercenary units recruited from outside the Empire.

The early Christian faith was rich in Roman ritual but promoted a code of life based on individual belief and the community of man and his environment. This moral code was compatible with the existing moral code of a pastoral people. In later years the faith of Christ became a formal church, and as early as the 7th century was showing clear signs of developing into a means of mass social control and oppression.

In the twilight days of the Empire the Pennine peoples embraced Christianity — there is evidence from the Wall that other faiths were suppressed at this time. The warriors of Rheged, Strathclyde, Elmet and Craven who fought the Angles of eastern Yorkshire saw themselves as Christian defenders of an ancient faith against paganism. From its stronghold in the Pennines Celtic Christianity established itself throughout Wales and Ireland.

In the 6th century the Picts and other peoples north of the Wall joined the Celtic Christian community. By the time of St. Augustine's mission to England, the alliance between Rheged and Northumbria had introduced the faith to the Anglian pagans of Yorkshire. Despite all that has been lost, a thread of belief still links Brigantia with the present day, to be at one, to be a warrior.

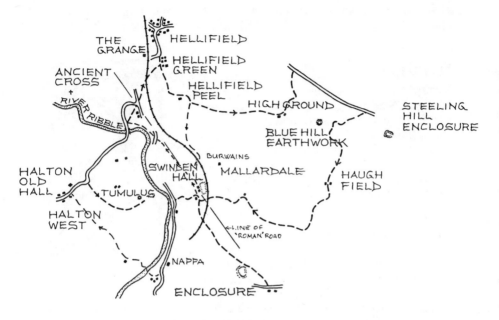

WALK 1

LOST ROAD & PEEL TOWER

8½ miles, 6¼ miles & 3 miles.
Hellifield — Swinden — Halton 4 hours.
Hellifield — Steeling Hill — Swinden 3 hours.
Hellifield — Swinden 2 hours.

MAP: *O.S. SD 85/95 PATHFINDER SERIES*
LUNCH: *Black Horse, Hellifield.*

Hidden amidst the drumlins of south Craven are a number of Ribblesdale villages and hamlets. Today our walk starts in Hellifield, once a busy railway junction and cattle mart, now a sleepy settlement resting from its former hustle and bustle. Within this restful and rustic setting we shall discover some of the lost gems that today's traveller overlooks in his/her rush to nowhere.

Old roadways whose origins are lost to the mists of time are trod again, a perilous river crossing is undertaken and with fortifications and tales of Scots raids this wander has much to offer. So without further ado let's be on our way.

Hellifield

Hellifield's oldest resident is the strange stone figure of 'Sheela-na-gig'. This odd stone carving was found in a garden serving as an ornament in 1967. It is 20ins. high and of coarse gritstone. Sheela-na-gig is a term which applies to figures which are often obscene and which have been found in some numbers in Ireland. Celtic in origin, but their precise significance has so far eluded scholars.

The Railway Station at Hellifield is worth a visit, a Victorian masterpiece of ironwork that is complete in every way. Built by the Midland Railway Company, the castings bear their sign of the dragon and the initials M.R. At the time of writing, November 25th 1989, the steam trains have returned along with the enthusiasts who today crowd the platforms, while overhead a flock of Whooper Swans fly in from Iceland or Spitzbergan to make their winter home on the flood plains between Long Preston and Settle.

The Black Bull at Hellifield makes for a good resting stop when our walk is done.

Hellifield to Hellifield Peel

From the Black Horse follow the road on to sharp bend (notice barn doorhead on left dated 1691 with the initials I.P.I.) and continue directly on to follow park driveway on to Hellifield Peel farm gate. Follow track on left to go through gate at the north east of Peel.

Hellifield Peel

Hellifield Peel stands in its modest park and is at the time of writing in a most ruinous condition. A sad situation for one of the oldest and most important structures in the Wapentake of Stancliffe and Newcross. In its present form the Peel consists of a roughly rectangular pile of three stories. The north and south fronts display re-modelling of the 18th century and later, but a closer

■ C 14
▨ C 15?
▤ C 17
▦ C 18 & later

0   5   10 metres
0   25 ft

examination of the building (see plan) will reveal at least three earlier phases of construction.

The earliest section of the present edifice is the rectangular block at the east end. This structure was originally built as a solar tower to an earlier timber-framed aisled hall in the 14th century. Evidence for the timber hall is the weathering of its steeply pitched roof, still plainly visible on the external face of the east wall of the tower.

Access to each floor of the tower was by a stair-turret at the north-east corner. The hall and tower structure would have looked similar to the tower and nave of a mediaeval church.

The ground floor of the solar block is a riot of fallen debris. The section of basement south of the collapsed stack has had a barrel vault, the toothing of which remains visible on the side walls. In the basement was located a stone-faced draw well.

The first floor contained the solar proper and the remains of a mural fireplace can be found in the east wall. The solar was lit by a large window of three lights, the outline of

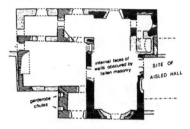

GROUND FLOOR

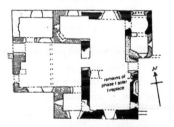

FIRST FLOOR

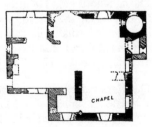

SECOND FLOOR

its jambs and pointed head can be seen externally around the Georgian sash window now occupying this position.

The second floor contained a domestic chapel of which the east window opening (a three-light mullion and transom window was inserted here in the 17th century and still remains) and piscina survive, the latter displaying an ogee-arched recess of 14th century form.

The timber hall seems to have been abandoned in the 15th century and the solar tower converted into a self-contained dwelling by enlarging the western end by the addition of two turrets (a Crown licence to crenellate and furnish with towers and battlements was granted to Laurence Hammerton in 1440).

During the 17th and 18th centuries the building was extended further to the west in the form that we see today.

The remains of a moat can still be made out encircling the site to the south and east. This is stone revetted on its inner face and was once linked up to a stream which flows from north to south to the west of the site. This ditch may have enclosed the earliest building that ever existed here.

The Early Yorkshire Charters inform us that the manor of Hellifield, like Gargrave, was divided between the honour of Skipton and the Percy fee, part of the Clifford fee going to Bolton Priory.

The Knights Hospitaller held the lands associated with the Peel of the Percy fee, and in the early 13th century the family of De Knoll held the manor from the Knights of St. John of Jerusalem and may be directly associated with building work at the Hellifield Peel site (the de Knolls gave name to Knowlmere Manor near Dunsop Bridge which they had also acquired at around this time).

The de Knolls held Hellifield till towards the end of the reign of Edward III (1312-77) when the last of the male line gave out leaving two daughters, Katherine and Anastasia, co-heirs to the family lands in Hellifield, Wigglesworth and Bolland. Katherine married Adam de Hammerton, Lord of Hammerton, and brought Hellifield into the hands of that family.

The Hammertons, in one form or another, held Hellifield Peel until the direct male line failed with the death of Chisnall Hammerton in 1908. Succession to Hellifield descended to his only daughter, Dorothy, who sold the Peel estate in 1948, from which time the house has been allowed to fall into ruin.

It would be fair to assume that the primary reason for the erection of a peel tower structure at Hellifield was as a defence for its holders against the Scots. Though built in the early 14th century, few in Craven would have forgotten the devastating raid on the region in 1138, when with great carnage William fitz Duncan laid waste the province. After Bannockburn, 1314, Scots raids became a common feature in the North of England.

Couple this with the internal problems that faced the reign of Edward II in the early 14th century — the Banastre Revolt of Northern Lords in 1315, and the Ordainers Rebellion of 1322 — and one can see many reasons for the emergence of fortified structures at that time. A secondary role would have been as a defence against cattle rustlers and local turmoil.

The most notable event recorded for the Peel is Sir Stephen Hammerton's involvement in the Pilgrimage of Grace of 1536 and his subsequent downfall. Sir Stephen was sought out by a group of some 300 rebels while hunting on 19 October, 1536. In fear of their threat to rule him for a change, and of the general disorder, he acted as one of their messengers dispatched to Skipton Castle to seek the support of the Earl of Cumberland in the rising. Thereafter he became fully embroiled, taking part in a campaign down the Ribble Valley and attending rebel gatherings at York and Pontefract, having been pardoned for his initial forced involvement.

When arrested he was taken for examination in the Tower of London whereupon he was charged with conspiracy against the king and a trial followed in Westminster Hall on 16 May 1537. He first pleaded not guilty but was 'persuaded' to change his plea. Having been found guilty he was executed at Tyburn on 25 May, 1537, but being a knight he was merely hanged and beheaded. Shortly after, his only son Henry died of grief over his father's fate. In 1538, Christopher Aske bequeathed his goods at Hellifield Peel to Roger Hammerton, reputedly one of Sir Stephen's nephews.

Hellifield Peel to Swinden Hall, via Steeling Hill

After observing the east wall of the Peel follow the track up, through gate (look back to see fully the moat around the Peel) and on to follow line of old trackway along the brow of the hill to pass through wall-gate. Walk directly on along the hillside to gated farm driveway. Pass through gate on left and follow right-hand boundary on to farm lane. Left, and follow lane to roadway. Right, and follow road on to go up the first farm lane on the right to Middle

Field Hill Farm. Pass over cattle-grid to follow track on right, through cattle-pens into small field. Walk on, through gate and follow wall up Blue Hill. The ancient ringwork is over on the right at the summit. Steeling Hill is the one directly to the east.

Steeling Hill Earthwork

On Steeling Hill, a high round knoll above Coniston Cold commanding one of the most central and extensive views in Craven, is an oval ditched earthwork with a circumference of 522 feet enclosing an area of three quarters of an acre. The plan is regular and has an entrance at the east, but the profiles of the ditch and outer bank are very slight. A Romano-British origin is ascribed to this structure, possibly a signal station of some kind.

The hill stands above Coniston Moor where tradition holds that the inhabitants of the Gargrave district made a stand against the Scottish invaders at Sweet Gap (north west of Coniston Moor) in Coniston and were cut down almost to a man. The same destroyers are supposed to have burnt to the ground six of Gargrave's seven churches (chapels and churches dependent on Gargrave). The Steeling Hill enclosure is said to be the Gargrave mens' rallying station.

Whitaker, in his 'History of Craven', saw the earthwork as Danish in origin — 9th/10th century.

Upon Blue Hill is another ancient enclosure, an earthen ditched ringwork. Its purpose and origin are again uncertain, it may or may not be related to the Steeling Hill earthwork.

Coniston Cold Stone Head

Built into the gable wall of a roadside barn on the west side of the village of Coniston Cold is a stone head of Celtic type.

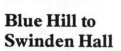

Blue Hill to Swinden Hall

Continue to follow the wall on to pass through corner gate. Left, and on to go over fence-stile. Follow left-hand fence on to farm lane, right and follow lane on to Haugh Field Farm *(notice the many old field boundaries and hollow-ways of long gone trackways around here). Pass through the main farmyard and down to go left between cow sheds and on to go through wall gate (gatepost inscribed R. IS.).*

Right, and follow wall to corner and on to next corner. Follow pathway on round through the little valley and on up to go through gateway (old windpump). Walk over to the right to go over low fence (horse jump) and follow old trackway down and on up past the barn to go through gateway. Follow left-hand fence-line on and down to farm lane. Left, and follow lane on to Swinden and the Hall.

Hellifield Peel to Swinden Hall

Pass through the field gate and follow right-hand fence on to go over corner fence-stile and across the field to go through gateway. (Burwains Barn is up in front of you). Follow track on to go under railway and on round to enter Swinden Hall farmyard. Walk on to front of Hall.

Swinden Hall

Swinden Hall is an outstandingly delightful building, completely symmetrical, three storeys with a central gabled porch, a wonderful mix of sandstone and limestone. The doorhead bears the date 1657, but only scratched on along with the following: MAYT HELb EWA NdHW. To what these letters refer I do not know. Another decorated doorhead can be found above the rear door. As with Halton West, Swinden Hall belonged to the Talbots of Bashall until 1660.

Between Swinden Hall and the railway embankment is what has been described as a Roman camp (E. E. Gregory BSJ No. 1. Vol 3. 1910). In plan it is a long rectangle being about 150 yards from north to south, and 90 yards east to west. The earthwork consists of a rampart of earth which contains a number of large stones (Gregory took these to be the remains of the camp wall) and outside of this is a ditch, both of which are in a very good state of preservation. There is no doubt in my mind that the earthwork represents the moated site of the former timber Hall at Swinden — pre 17th century.

Gregory also put forward the existence of a Roman road running through the lands of Swinden Hall en route to Long Preston. Others since have kept this avenue of thought open, including Professor Raistrick. Gregory also thought that another road crossed this just to the south of the Hall.

The Swinden to Long Preston section of this supposed Roman road is best made out running between the Hall and Goosemere Height, clearly visible for half a mile or so. Proceeding north west from Swinden Hall the road forded Mansell Beck to follow the fence-line to Goosemere Height.

A typical section shows that the roadway was 6 yards wide, cambered in the centre, and well made. It is sunk to around 18 inches below the level of the surrounding ground, and has a parallel bank or earthwork on either side; many stones may be seen in each bank.

This road he took to run between Elslack and Long Preston Roman forts. The other two roads that branch east and west from the one above described he thought ran to the north of Slaidburn to join the 'Salter Track' Roman Road, and the Roman Villa at Gargrave respectively.

During February 1989, members of the Pendle Heritage Centre Archaeological Group discovered what they hold to be a new southern section of Gregory's 'Roman road', but instead of seeing it as heading to Elslack, they view it as leading to Barnoldswick to join the Brogden Lane Roman Road there. The PHCAG 'Roman Road' is situated between Horton and Swinden below Stoop Hill. This road is around 16 feet wide with a ditch on either side, cambered in the centre.

In my view PHCAG's work here is highly commendable, a remarkable piece of field work. It is the work of groups like PHCAG that help us all to piece together the 'jig-saw' of our ancient past — they deserve full support in their efforts.

To the north east of Swinden Hall is a field barn named 'Burwains', locally pronounced "Burrins". The name refers to a borran or cairn and is cognate with Old English 'byrgan' — "to bury". It is a name often given to an ancient burial mound or to some long lost buried structure — Elslack Roman fort was formerly known as Burwen Castle. The Burwains place-name here may also refer to some ancient burial mound or other earthwork in the area of Mallardale.

Looking over to the west from Swinden Hall one can clearly see Round Hill Tumulus, with its wooded backdrop, in the grounds of Halton Place.

Swinden Camp

Upon the hillside to the south east of Swinden Hall, at Swinden Moor Head, is an earthwork known as Swinden Camp. It is an oval ditched earthwork of 1½ acres, lying in a shallow valley and intersected by a stream. The precise nature and origin of the structure has not yet been determined, but thought to be of a pre-Conquest date.

If you wish to visit Swinden Camp, then follow the roadway through Swinden and the old lane on, through gate, and on over the rise to pass under the railway. Once through the gate cross the stream and climb the banking to a very low wall. Walk up the hill, between two large trees and on up to the right of the summit and into the shallow valley.

Next described is the short route back to Hellifield following the 'Roman' road. This is followed by directions to Nappa and Halton West and should only be attempted in dry months as Nappa ford can be rather precarious at times:

Swinden Hall to Hellifield
via Halton Bridge

Walk down by the side of the Hall and cow sheds to go through gate. Follow trackway on, across the ford and on up to follow right-hand fence on (the 'Roman road' runs parallel to this path on the other side of the fence) to go over corner fence-stile. Follow track on then drop down to the left onto the roadway. Go through gap in fence opposite and follow path to the right through the wood to go over stile. Follow river up to Halton Bridge.

With your back to the road, walk across the field up to the left to go through gate at road junction. Cross junction to go over wall-stile and walk over to the left to go over fence-stile. Walk over to the right to go under railway and through gate. Cross the field, heading up to the left to go over wall-stile onto lane. Left, and walk on to the Black Bull at Hellifield.

Swinden Hall to Nappa

Walk on and follow the lane down to the right to roadway. Left, and follow the road on to Nappa. Follow the lane down to the Hipping stones.

Nappa

Nappa, along with Newsholme, belonged once to the wealthy Hospital of St. Leonard at York. The manor was granted to Arthur Darcy, and Thomas Darcy, his brother had licence to alienate the same to Richard Cutts in 1582 (Elizabeth I).

There are many fine 17th century houses and farmsteads to be found in Nappa and Newsholme. The whitewashed farm just up on the roadway is a good example. Here we find two doorheads dated 1678, with the initials S.P. & S.E.P.

Nappa to Halton West Old Hall

Walk past the cottages down to the river and cross the hipping stones. Walk into small group of trees to go through gateway at rear. Pass through the small gate on the right and walk up the hill to follow left-hand fence around to Nappa Flats cottage, via gate.

Follow the old trackway and right-hand fence to go through gateway. Cross the field on a slight right diagonal to go over gated cattle-bridge. Walk directly on to go through field gate. Cross the field on a right diagonal to the right of the farm buildings to go over wall-stile. Pass through yard onto roadway. The Old Hall is over on the right.

Halton West

The village gave its name to the ancient family of Haltons, the last heiress of whom, in 1483, added it to the great estate of the Talbots of Bashall (near

Clitheroe). The land remained in Talbot hands until their extinction in c.1660, after which Thomas Yorke purchased the Halton estate. He built Halton Place and enhanced the area greatly making many judicious improvements.

During this time the Old Hall was reduced to a simple farmstead, but it still displays its early 17th century frontage. Other farmhouses in the hamlet have mullioned windows and doorheads from the same period.

In the grounds of Halton Place, upon Round Hill, is a Bronze Age burial mound that has yielded an urn burial. A trackway from the road leads to the Tumulus.

To the north of Halton West, above Broken Brow, stands the remains of an ancient cross on lands once owned by the Knights Hospitaller. In 1482 the Prior of Newland enjoined all the tenants of the hospitallers in Hellifield to erect crosses on their properties, so giving us a date for the remains.

Halton West to Hellifield

Follow the Hellifield road to go over Halton Bridge. Pass through gateway on right and walk across the field up to the left to go through gate at road junction. Cross the junction to go over wall-stile and walk over to the left to go over fence-stile. Walk over to the right to go under railway and through gate, then cross field heading left to go over wall-stile onto lane. Left, and follow lane on to the pub at Hellifield.

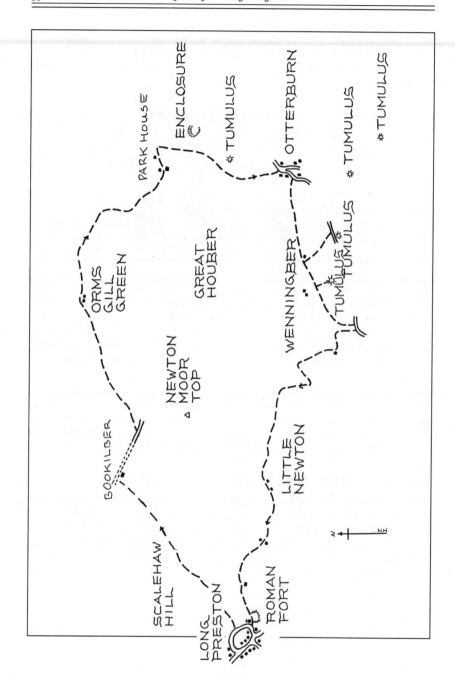

Walk 2

ROMAN FORT
AND
BURIAL MOUNDS

8½ miles, 4 hours, packed lunch or afternoon
meal at Boars Head back in Long Preston.

MAP: *O.S. OUTDOOR LEISURE 10.*
        Yorkshire Dales, Southern Area.

START: *Park your car at Long Preston railway station.*

Today we explore an ancient church and the surface features of a Roman fort, and between doing this we shall wander into the hilly landscape below the limestone scars of Settle and Malham. Here we shall discover hidden farming settlements tucked away in secret valleys, once the homes of Brigantian farmers and later, Scandinavian settlers. A very pleasurable and easy going walk through varied and rolling scenery.

Railway Station to St Mary the Virgin
Follow lane to village main street, right, then first left up to the church gates.

St Mary the Virgin, Long Preston
The present church, which for the most part is of the 14th century, the chancel was rebuilt in 1868 and the tower rebuilt in 1760, stands on the site of two earlier structures. We enter the church by the porch above whose doorway is a stone cross in the Irish style. Built into the wall of the porch is a mediaeval grave slab. Once inside the church all is very pleasing, only the chancel disappoints. The arcades are of four bays with tall octagonal piers with typical 14th century capitals and double-chamfered arches. The windows are mostly Decorated and of two lights.

On the south side of the altar, under the arch, is the Hammerton Tomb dated 1445. Laurence Hammerton then resided at Hellifield Peel. The piscina is set in the wall east of the tomb in the south sanctuary wall. The Hammerton Chapel is in the south aisle and built into the low north wall of this chapel is another mediaeval tombstone.

At the rear of the church is the font which is possibly Norman. The font cover is a wonderful piece, hexagonal, two tiers, and crocketed spire. It is dated 1726 with the initials of the church wardens of that time. Two Jacobean pieces inspire — the intricately carved pulpit and a chair by the north door dated 1695 with the initials B.P. Entry from the nave to the tower is through a small early 14th century doorway. A stairway leads up to the bell chamber and a strong vaulted chamber, about 6ft by 4ft, to which it is difficult to assign any use other than a strongroom.

The living was granted by Walter de Amunderville during the reign of Stephen (1135-1154), and he bestowed it upon the Church and Canon of the Priory and College of St. Cuthbert of Embsay before 1153. The Priory was transfered to Bolton Priory c.1160, and the Prior and Convent of Bolton became the patron of the living until the Reformation. After which the patronage was exercised by the Dean and Chapter of Christ Church, Oxford.

When the chancel was rebuilt in 1868 the foundations of a semicircular apse were revealed. This would have belonged to a Norman church, or even a much earlier building of a church that once stood here.

Signs of another building were discovered during the digging of graves near the entrance to the churchyard. What has been described as "a floor of painted tiles" was met with. 'Painted tiles' or a mosaic? Our early 19th century informant fails to specify. (Whitaker, in his "History of Craven", thought the tiles to be part of a Chapel to St. Michael referred to in a charter of 1431. This cannot be so given the nature of the floor find and probably refers to one of the church chapels, or was a mistake.) It is more likely that the 'painted' tile floor belongs to some 9th century structure, or even possibly to some Roman building, given the close proximity to the fort site.

The place-name 'Long Preston' may also give a clue. In the 1086 Norman Survey it is recorded as 'Prestune' where "Ulf had three carucates for geld, and one church", in 1066. So a church is recorded as standing here before the Conquest and it would be fair to assume that it had an Anglian foundation some time early in the 8th century. We strongly doubt that the painted tile floor belonged to any early church, and until future examination, its origins must remain a mystery.

Long Preston Parish Church to Orms Gill

Leave the churchyard to follow the lane to the right to the rear of the school. Follow the lane on the right on, past Hewitt House drive and along the trackway to go over footbridge. Follow path up to the left and on, following wall to go over wall-stile. Walk on to go over next wall-stile to follow the path up the hill to go over another wall-stile.

Follow path to the left to go over corner wall-stile and on towards Bookilber Farm to go over wall-stile. Cross the field to go over wall-stile onto trackway. Right, and follow the trackway on for some way to go over stile on left. Walk on up on a right-diagonal, passing wall corner and on down to cross stream then go over wall-stile. Follow path on heading up to the right to go over wall-stile near animal feeder. Cross the field directly to enter lane via corner gate. Right, and walk down to Orms Gill Green.

Orms Gill Green

What a wonderful hidden place this is, a green pasture secreted by a ring of hills. In such a place a Brigantian farmer would have built his homestead, and as the place-name informs us, some later Norwegian was to settle here too.

Orms Gill stands on an exposed outcrop of limestone that has provided a useful resource to past farmers. The robust limekiln stands over-grown above tumbling waters of the gill, resounding as they rush through the tunnel. A very pleasant place indeed.

Orms Gill to Park House

Follow the trackway on, and around to the right and on to go through field-gate on right before the trackway bends down to the left. Walk on, keeping left to go through field-gate. Walk directly on to enter Park House farmyard via gate.

Park House Earthworks

On the hillsides beyond Park House stand two ancient earthworks. The first that we shall pass is a circular ditched enclosure of two thirds of an acre standing in a prominent position on Park Hill above Otterburn Beck. The ditch and external bank have a very slight profile and are barely distinguishable in the field. A bronze spearhead and palstave were found near the site, all a feature of Bronze/Iron Age settlement in the area. Beyond the enclosure is a denuded tumulus, the remains of a Bronze Age burial mound. From the earthwork can be gained fine views over Pendle, Flasby Fell and Rylstone Fell.

Park House to Otterburn

Pass through the field-gate up on the left and follow trackway on to barn. Walk up the hill to corner of wall, turn right, and cross the field to go through gateway above wood (the enclosure is up on the left). Walk on and down to join farm track at gate. Follow track (the tumulus is the circular depression up on the left) on to Otterburn.

Otterburn

Otterburn is an old quarrying/farming community and owes much to the early 19th century, architecturally speaking, though a settlement is recorded here in 1086. The old villagers have long gone giving way to the ubiquitous cottage-commuter set.

Located around Otterburn are a number of Bronze Age burial mounds. One was excavated in 1885 by R H Tiddeman of H. M. Geological Survey. He found two urns, 12ins x 10¾ins & 10ins x 8ins, and an accessory cup. The urns were of overhanging collar type, but ornamented with dots only, lacking the common twisted thong ornament seen on other Airedale urns (the urns were of the type found at Pinder Hill, Waddington). Sadly the urns cannot now be traced.

In 1889 another mound was opened at Otterburn on Lingber Hill. The mound yielded two urns, each covered by a gritstone slab. The larger urn was 12ins high and contained a small bronze blade suggestive of a tanged and riveted dagger, a 3ins. sharp bone needle and an unidentifiable but riveted piece of metal. The smaller urn, approx. 10ins high, was badly broken and was on top of fragments of a third vessel which contained calcinated bones and an accessory cup.

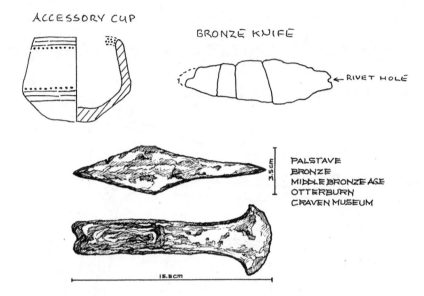

A bronze palstave was found some time ago at Otterburn. This is now on display at the Craven Museum, Skipton.

On entering the village notice the gateway of the second house on the left. Built into the wall by the gate is a carved stone head that probably came from some Victorian, now demolished, church.

Otterburn to Long Preston Roman Camp

Take the Hellifield Road through the village to enter gated farm lane on right. Follow track up for a short way then head into wood on left and follow left-hand wall on, over wall-stile and on to go over fence and wall-stiles. Walk directly on to go over stile above Wenningber Farm. Cross field to go over wall-stile. Walk up the hill to the left of the tree and down to follow Goal farm lane to roadway.

Right, and walk a few yards to go through gate on right. Follow left-hand fence on to barn then head over to the right to go through gate on left. Follow trackway on to enter Haw Lane via field-gate. Left, and follow lane on to go through field-gate on the right. Cross the field on a right-diagonal to corner of wall and follow wall on to go over wall-stile on left.

Cross the moor on a right-diagonal to enter Little Newton farmyard lane at sheep pens (Newton is also mentioned as a settlement in the Domesday Survey). Follow the lane on to the rear gate or the churchyard. The Roman fort and road are over on the left.

Roman Camp, Long Preston

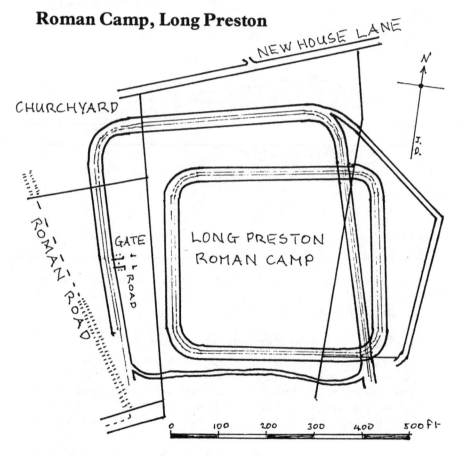

A Roman fort/temporary camp was first discovered at Long Preston in the 1920's. It is positioned on the Roman road between Ilkley and Overborough, about half way between the two, on an almost flat piece of land which becomes precipitous to the south. The layout of the larger fort is unconventional. The crooked southern side is due to following the edge of the steep slope to the beck, and the single fosse here is quite small. This branches from the eastern and western fosses, which have been cut straight through to the steep southern slope. These each have an angle near their centres. A western gate was examined enough to prove the existence of a double entrance with rather small and irregularly placed post-holes containing no wood. The intravallum road was found in good condition.

This small excavation yielded several pieces of coarse pottery, a mortarium and what was said to be window glass. Only the outline of the smaller fort was determined. The ramparts examined were seen to have been of clay on a cobble foundation. Since the 1920's no further work has been done on the site.

The larger earlier fort is probably Agricolan or Flavian in origin, and the eastern 'extension' may be an enclosure for camp followers. The later inner fort still awaits examination to determine its origin and purpose.

Field Walls around Long Preston

The lane we followed from Long Preston towards Orms Gill Green, Scalehaw Lane, is constructed for the most part of river-bed cobbles, an unusual feature of the area. By the time we reached Orms Gill the familiar limestone slab-walling dominates.

Long Preston stands upon the South Craven Fault — Millstone Grit to the east, limestone to the south and west, and Great Scar Limestone to the far north. The area between Long Preston and Skipton is dominated by an extensive area of drumlins.

This swarm of glacial deposit was the result of a burst in a dammed ribbon lake that once stood between Long Preston and Settle. This moraine-dammed lake was left behind after the ice retreat in the late Pleistocene period. The rounded stones here would have been formed by long lost rivers to the south, dragged back by the ice sheet and later deposited in the Settle/Long Preston lake, upon whose burst they were released and scattered in the surrounding landscape.

So you see, even simple stones have their travel stories to tell.

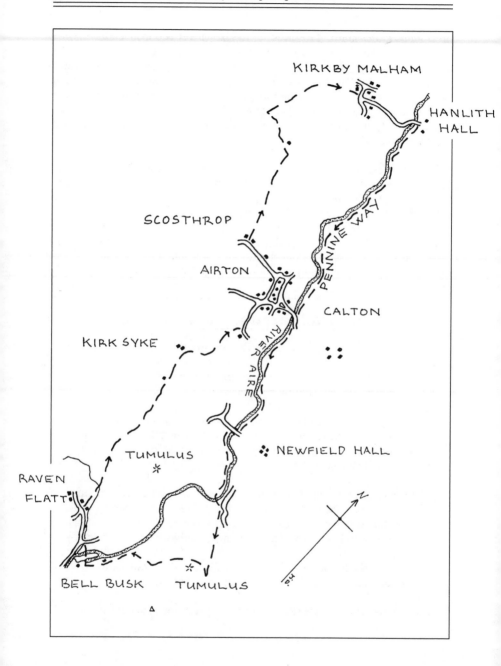

Walk 3

AIREDALE HAMLETS

7½ miles.

Car parking by Kirkby Malham church.

MAP: *O.S. OUTDOOR LEISURE 10.*
Yorkshire Dales, Southern Area.

LUNCH OR
EVENING MEAL: *The Victoria, Kirkby Malham.*

This is a good morning or afternoon walk that allows one to discover the often passed-by hamlets of Airedale; settlements hardly changed over the last one hundred years, linked together by narrow back-roads and lanes. The valley floor is a haven for plant and bird life, many species of wader have established breeding grounds here, so avoid noise and keep to the footpaths. The history revealed is varied ranging from the earliest times up to the beginnings of the Industrial Revolution, a hidden tapestry one might say. So without further ado let's be on our way.

St. Michael the Archangel

Kirkby Malham parish contains seven civil parishes in it and a foundation that goes back to the Norsemen; St. Michael the Archangel was a popular dedication in areas under their dominance. The church first comes to mention in 1199, when Adam de Giggleswick gave it to the Abbot and Canons of the Abbey of Our Lady at West Dereham, Norfolk. It remained in their hands up to the 16th century Reformation.

The church had a major restoration between 1879-81, the main cost being borne by the then patron, Walter Morrison of Malham

Tarn, friend of Charles Kingsley, creator of "The Water Babies", inspiration for which was gained hereabouts.

Near the top of the south-east tower buttress is carved the coat of arms of Fountains Abbey which held much of the land in the parish from Malham northwards, Bolton Priory held land east of the River Aire, and West Dereham Abbey held large areas of land to the west. On the south-west buttress are four coats of arms; Malham of Calton, Tempest of Bracewell, Unknown, and Bank of Bank Newton.

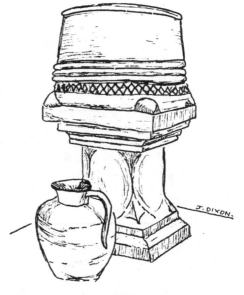

Inside the church we find a primitive, circular Norman font with familiar dog-tooth ornamentation, standing on a modern pedestal. The next thing that one notices are the seven image niches on the piers which once held figures of Our Lord, Our Lady, St. Nicholas, St. Syth, St. Sonday (Dominic) and two unknown Saints. Two 'Celtic' stone heads can be observed on the north arcade and may have belonged to an earlier building.

The four family high pews, which date from 1631 to 1723 bear the initials or names of their original owners. The box pews are probably later Georgian. The oak chest at the back of the nave is said to date from the 14th century. This was a muniment chest and once held documents such as charters, rights and privileges for safe keeping. By the side of the font are a number of 13th century gravemarkers, very richly decorated.

The vestry contains old photographs of the church, and a key to the coats of arms on the sanctuary panelling. The photos include Captain James King of this parish who brought Captain Cook's ship "The Endeavour" home after the explorer's murder in Hawaii.

By the lych-gate stand the village stocks, and nearby a cross base is all that remains of some ancient cross. The Vicarage is three-storeyed with a three-storeyed porch dated 1622.

Kirkby Malham to Airton Bridge

From The Victoria Inn follow the Hanlith Road (cottage dated 1637, and barn dated c.1667 A.) down to the river bridge. Cross bridge and over stile on right (Pennine Way). Follow river down to Airton Bridge.

Calton

The eastern road from the bridge leads to the tiny hamlet of Calton, the birthplace of Major General Lambert, who, holding several important posts under Oliver Cromwell, and being responsible for the capture of Bradford, eventually died while still a prisoner of the Crown.

Major General John Lambert was one of the great 'would have beens' of British history, a Colonel in the New Model Army who held many important posts during the Commonwealth. Though Cromwell provided Britain with one of its best periods of administration during the 17th century, in one key area he failed. The existence of the English Republic was dependent on his own personality and the loyalty of the army.

Major General Lambert

When Cromwell died, the government of the Republic was thrown into crisis. This crisis came to a head when General Monk, Commander of the Army in Scotland, declared for Charles II and began his march south. At this stage Lambert was thrust into the centre of the political stage.

On behalf of the Council of the Commonwealth, Lambert gathered regiments from the south-east of England and began to march north to intercept Monk. His march north was slow and indecisive — as he moved north, political panic spread in the City of London. By the time he reached the north Lambert could only surrender to the forces of the King.

Charles Stewart, a drunkard and womaniser, was restored to the throne and a witch-hunt of former Commonwealth officials was unleashed. The wealthy were able to purchase pardons, and the poor were taken to the gallows. Lambert was a man of modest means, but he did avoid the gallows only to face a life sentence.

At first Lambert was imprisoned in Guernsey and, like many men unjustly imprisoned, he found solace in religion. For many years he cultivated the gardens he had laid out within the castle. In the 1660's, as a final act of vengeance, Lambert was transferred from his beloved gardens to a cell on a dank island off Plymouth harbour. In the last year of his life he was visited by the King and the Duke of York. He would not ask forgiveness and was not pardoned. He died at peace with his God, a political prisoner and Commonwealth man to the end.

Had he marched north in 1659, as Cromwell would have done — with vigour and decision, and crushed Monk, he, like Cromwell, could have been a Protector of England, and the disastrous reign of Charles II could have been avoided.

Calton Hall was built by the General's son, John, the older Hall having been burnt down soon after the Restoration. A stone pillar in the front garden bears the inscription IL 1688 WF 1688. The Lamberts' connection with Calton dates from 1516, when John Lambert the elder, a lawyer, leased the manor and hall from John Malham. This John Lambert held many Crown offices and benefited from the Dissolution of the Monasteries. At the height of their prosperity the Lamberts held most of Malhamdale.

Airton Bridge to Haw Crag Tumulus

Follow 'Pennine Way' riverside path on down to Newfield Bridge. Cross bridge to go over stile on left and follow river down (Flasby Fell comes into view) to go over footbridge. Follow path to go over stile then follow trackway up to top of field to go through gate over on the left. Walk directly on to the ditched bowl barrow.

Haw Crag Tumulus

Here we find a fine example of a ditched bowl barrow, one of many Bronze Age barrows to be found in this part of Airedale. An urn of the Pennine Type with accessory cup was found during excavation, similar to those found at nearby Otterburn. The barrow sits on the side of a rise some way from the distinctive summit of Haw Crag, a limestone outcrop that offers outstanding panoramic views over Craven: Kirkby Fell, Hawkswick Clowder, Malham

Moor, Cracoe & Rylstone Fell, Flasby Fell and the South Craven moorlands with Pendle all come into vision.

Haw Crag Tumulus to Bell Busk

Walk over to the right to pass through wall opening and follow left-hand wall on to go through gateway, then follow wall down to riverbank via gate. Follow river down and pass through farmyard then down the farm-track to roadway. Right, over Aire and Otterburn Bridges to follow Bell Busk road to Raven Flatt and Bell Busk.

Bell Busk

In the days before the intrusion of the motor car, Bell Busk was a rail halt and starting point for visitors into Malhamdale who would proceed by foot or wagonette to the Cove region. Today few visit this out-of-the-way hamlet, those who do discover the old post office with adjacent stone cottages, the 17th century Raven Flatt farm and the old water mill below the river bridges.

Bell Busk to Airton

Take the bridleway below Raven Flatt and follow it over bridge and past barn to leave track to follow left-hand fence on to go through gate. Follow path to the right, through gate and on past barn and through gate to follow trackway on to roadway. Left, and walk on into Airton.

 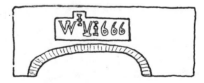

Airton

Airton is a pleasant village sited around a triangular green on which stands just one cottage with its stone-walled garden. The Post Office, Vipoint House, is dated 1666 with the initials W. I. V., but the Friends' Meeting House, dated 1700, is more interesting. This latter building was built by William Ellis (whose own cottage of the same period is immediately opposite) and is still owned by the Society of Friends and used for occasional Meetings for Worship. It was converted in 1940 into a wartime evacuee hostel and today is a Holiday Hostel, ideal for family, school or club groups of up to 12 people (Tel: 072 93 263, Mr & Mrs Parker).

Other dated houses can be found in the village. By the river we find the old cotton mill, now converted into dwellings, that once provided employment for the surrounding villages. In mediaeval times a few linen weavers lived at Airton and Calton. In the latter half of the 18th century cotton was introduced and a new mill was built by the beck on the site of a former corn mill. It was rebuilt by Dewhursts in 1838.

The stone head pictured here is in use as decoration above the door of a dwelling house and it has no other history. It is carved from sandstone and is 8 ins. high with flat back, a squarish nose, and eyes with upper and lower lids joined in ovals.

AIRTON
SD. 9059

On our way out of the village we pass Scosthrop Manor dated 1686 on the gabled porch, and 1603 over the inner doorway. The doorway lintel has decoration with two semicircles.

Airton to Kirkby Malham

Take the Settle Road out of the village and follow it on past Scosthrop House and cottages to enter the first farmyard on the right. Walk on to go between farm buildings to footpath sign. Take the 'Kirkby Malham' footpath that goes through the gate and up the field to go over corner wall-stile.

Follow the wall on and cross field directly to go over wall-stile, on and over next wall-stile. Follow wall on, over stile and on (Kirkby Fell and Malham Cove come into view) down the field to go over fence-stile near barn. Follow trackway up to the left and across top field to go through gate. Follow wall down to the right to go over wall-stile.

Walk down to cross stream and walk directly up the field (yellow markers) to go over stile by wood. Follow fence down to go over stile, right, and on to go over wall-stile. Walk down to the left to go through gate and on down to cross stream. Walk on to the churchyard.

Kirkby Malham & Hanlith

After lunching in The Victoria, dated GS 1840, a wander round the village to view the many fine stone houses would be a grand little tour. Many of the houses bear 17th century dated doorheads, some pictured here.

Seeing the village today it is hard to believe that it was once the seat of industry: Scargill Mill, on the site of the ancient corn mill and the Vicarage were once both used for cotton spinning; and a bobbin mill stood by the beck. Scargill Mill can still be found between Kirkby and Hanlith up a lane by the Aire river.

Hanlith is a tiny hamlet dominated by Hanlith Hall, one time hall of the Sarjeantsons, an ancient Malhamdale family. The present house was first built in 1668 by Robert Sarjeantson and remodelled in 1829 and 1912.

The original doorway, inscribed RS 1668, has survived and in the gable a large stone figure in relief of a serjeant holding a halberd can be seen. A halberd is carved on each side of the doorway representing the holder of a mediaeval manor who held his land by giving a personal service to his lord. Ingham Lodge in Ribblesdale and New Hall near Settle also have this feature.

I left behind the crowd of men,
The towns with smoky pall,
And sought the hills of old Brigantia,
To breathe the air of freedom.

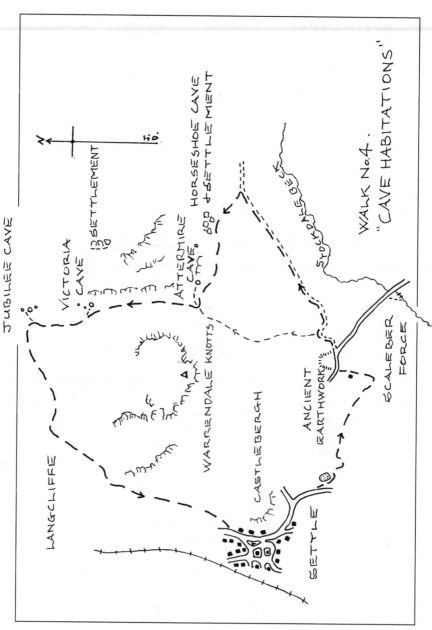

Walk 4

CAVE HABITATIONS

7 miles.

MAP: *O.S. OUTDOOR LEISURE 10.*
Yorkshire Dales, Southern Area.

LUNCH: *Naked Man Cafe or any pub in Settle.*

With the advent of a motor by-pass, Settle has returned once again to being a quaint Ribblesdale market town, dominated as always by the towering lime-stone mass of Castleberg. The area that we shall explore today holds some of the most dramatic scar scenery in Britain, a long succession of rugged Great Scar Limestone.

It is amongst this sea-bed landscape that we shall discover signs of man's most ancient past in an age when Britain was still a part of the Continental main-land, the age of large mammals and inland lakes, of nomadic hunters amid the tundra of glacial retreat.

So now we set forth and climb up to a true 'lost world' on the highfolds that form the Craven Backdrop — an adventure to the mind and eye.

This walk can be started at Settle to follow the main route,

DOORWAY OF THE FOLLY, AT SETTLE.

or alternatively the town may be avoided by parking your car in the lay-by near the 'ancient earthwork' north-west of Scaleber Force allowing for a full exploration of the upland limestone landscape.

The Folly, Settle

High Street leads to The Folly, a large and ambitious town house of three storeys with recessed centre and two wings. It is the doorway, with its fantastic surround of Gothic forms, that the eye finally descends on, remarkable for the date of 1679.

The house, also known as Tanner House, was built for Thomas Preston.

Settle to Ancient Earthwork

Walk behind the Market Square "Shambles" and follow the Kirkby Malham road up to the right on up Albert Hill to take the right fork at Chapel House. Follow lane on to take the left fork up through gateway to go through top gate. Left, and follow wall up to follow top wall to the right then at corner opening head up left to go over wall-stile. Follow track over to the left to follow left-hand wall on, over wall-stile and on to enter Lambert Lane track via gate. Left and walk on to roadway. The earthwork is in the field opposite.

Ancient Earthwork

On the north side of High Hill Lane where it meets Stockdale Lane is a large earthen structure. It is about 350ft. long by 250ft. wide, and has a surrounding ditch and bank. Old maps refer to earthwork as a 'Roman Camp' or 'Ancient Earthwork'. Its form assigns it to the Romano-British period, a defensive or industrial site. Only archaeological investigation will determine its true purpose, possibly a monastic stock enclosure.

If you have used the lay-by here as your starting point and wish to explore the uplands only, then we suggest that you follow the following directions to Attermire Scar:

Follow the lane on the left round to go over wall-stile. Follow the path on between High and Sugar Loaf Hills to enter a truly magnificent otherworld landscape of limestone reef knolls and scar landscape. Work your way via wall-stile over to the right and on to wall opening (notice the earthen mound and large cast iron plates, the remains of a Woods shooting target of 1860, used by the local militia). Pass through the wall opening and follow the scree track up and on up to a grassy ledge that leads one along to Attermire Cave. The cave can be followed in for some way in complete safety with the aid of a torch.

Ancient Earthwork to Scaleber Force

Follow roadway round to the right to go over wall-stile on the right at wood. Follow pathway on to view Scaleber Force.

Scaleber Force

The waters of Stockdale Beck come down off the moor and gather under Scaleber Bridge to tumble over the Force and a series of smaller falls, all hidden in a delightful wooded glen.

Many bronze implements have been found in the area around Scaleber, and at Cleatop Park, just over the hill, a stone circle once existed. Sadly, the circle has been destroyed.

Scaleber Force to Horseshoe Settlement

Walk back along the road to go right, up Stockdale Lane, passing the wall-stile and on up to go through corner gate at footpath sign. Follow the wallside path to the left to go through wall-gate. Walk up to the right to an area of disturbed ground that was once an ancient British settlement.

Horseshoe Settlement

The foundations of dwellings with their adjacent enclosures and auxiliary structures can be clearly made out in the grasses. Finds from the site point to occupation from the Iron Age through into the Roman period, weaving and domestic items being most common.

The site is located above the eastern end of an old lake bed, now a mire from which Attermire takes its name, and may have been occupied in the early post-glacial period.

Horseshoe Settlement to Attermire Cave

Follow path on to go through two gates and on to near wall opening, then follow a scree track back up to the right on up to a grassy ledge that leads on along to the cave.

FIBULA + BROOCHES

Attermire Cave

Attermire Cave was used as a hiding place for personal possessions in the troubled 3rd and 4th centuries A.D. (see Victoria Cave), their owners never returning to recover their wealth. Along with pottery, and other domestic items, finds from the site include coins, bronze wire fibula, two large brooches both of gold on bronze and a dismantled chariot.

The find of the vehicle has led some to view the site as the burial spot of some Romano-British warrior, and this interpretation cannot be ruled out.

Attermire Cave has a length of some 550 ft, and almost bisects the scars. One can walk in for the first 60 ft. then it requires a crawl for 20 ft. and on to enter a pool chamber 160 ft. from the entrance some 40ft. high. After descending a stalagmite staircase a high passage continues for 150 ft. Here a small hole on the west side leads to a narrow passage. After a traverse it opens out into the final chamber.

Attermire Cave to Victoria Cave

Return down the track (do not go through opening) and follow wall up to the right to join scarside track and on, over wall-stile and then work your way up to the right to the large mouth of the cave.

Victoria Cave

Victoria Cave is located in a cliff of carboniferous limestone known as Kings Scar, to the east above the town of Settle. The cave contains three large irregular chambers with a single entrance facing south-west. Excavations at the mouth of the cave to a depth of 12ft. have revealed worked flints and several stag-antler implements.

Two pieces of antler had been shaped into cylindrical rods and may have once tipped a fish lance/harpoon. Another is of a distinctive shape having broad barbs on either side. In form it is similar to the Azilian harpoons of northern Spain, named after the cave of Mas d'Azil in the Pyrenees, and to harpoons found in north-west Scotland.

These tools are attested to upper palaeolithic man, hunters of Late Glacial times of the Magdalenian tradition, whose territory was centred on France and northern Spain These tools show that the direct ancestors of modern man had reached the north of England by c.10,000 B.C. (prior to c.5,000 B.C., Britain was still joined to the Continent).

Prior to the arrival of man the cave had been home to cave bear and hyena who would have lived upon the then open tundra along with horse, hare and reindeer.

Other finds from the cave show intermittent occupation by later Mesolithic hunters, and in the troubled times of the 3rd and 4th centuries A,D. it provided a refuge for Romano-British peoples.

By the middle of the 3rd century A.D. sea raiders were becoming sufficiently persistent for the Emperor Diocletian to establish a branch of the Roman navy to deal with the threat. Its first commander was Carausius, who used the force for his own ends and declared himself Emperor of Britain in 287. Six years later he was murdered by Allectus, who then himself usurped the throne. The military presence in Northern Britain was greatly reduced at this time as Allectus gathered his forces for a confrontation with Constantius in 296 from whom he suffered defeat.

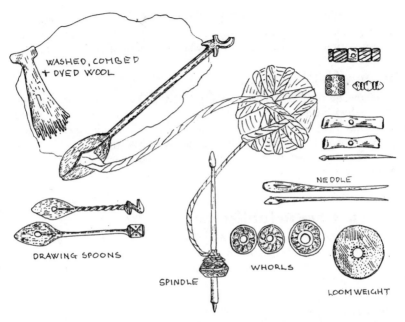

WASHED, COMBED + DYED WOOL

NEDDLE

DRAWING SPOONS

SPINDLE

WHORLS

LOOM WEIGHT

During these upheavals the northern tribes again seized an opportunity to sweep south. Hoards of coins etc, hidden away, but never recovered from caves such as Victoria, well document these troubled times. Coins recovered from the caves around Settle span the period 253-75 A.D., and along with pottery, bronze brooches, domestic textile equipment, armlets and jet and glass beads add up to the possessions of some native family forced to hide their wealth from hostile tribesmen.

All the cave sites in the area are adjacent to groups of small crofts and fields, usually with traces of hutments. Near to the mouths of the caves there is generally a sheltered platform with abundant charcoal hearth sites on which much of the pottery was found.

At Jubilee and Attermire Caves the outer platform is less well marked than Victoria and the cave itself is a series of ramifying passages, narrow and often of great height only occasionally opening into a chamber large enough to provide refuge. In normal times it would be fair to see the caves as shepherds shelters, but it would be very wrong to see them as family occupation sites in themselves. Perhaps in some cases a wooden structure stood on the entrance platforms, the occupants utilizing the cave as a rear store.

Victoria Cave has a length of 450 ft. and rope and caving gear are needed for a full exploration. Wet Cave is located under the scree below Victoria Cave. This is a natural fissure cave and can be walked for most of the 60 ft. length.

Victoria Settlement

Excavations on the settlement site above Victoria Cave revealed an elongated bowl lined with clay and containing around 1 cwt. of barytes. This impure baryte contained a good deal of malachite and some haematite, a carbonate of copper and iron oxide respectively; slag and charcoal were also found. The nearby circular hutments yielded more barytes and the site is thought to represent a Romano-British metal-working site given the close proximity to mineral ores.

Victoria Cave to Jubilee Cave

Make your way back to the path and follow it on (Ingleborough and Pen-Y-Ghent come into view and dominate the skyline, each competing for the eye) to go over wall-stile. Follow the trackway on and around to the right to Jubilee Cave.

Jubilee Cave

Excavations at Jubilee Cave have produced material similar to and contemporary with that found in Victoria and Attermire Caves. But Jubilee differs in that it contained a large number of Iron Age burials.

Most of the skeletons were found carefully tucked away along the sides of passages, generally under an overhanging ledge, or thrust down into some deeper fissure in the side passages. One skeleton was wearing a necklace made from the perforated teeth of a wolf. With all the burials there was nothing resembling a made grave, though in most cases artefacts are either with or very near to the skeleton.

Cave burials were also found in Dowkerbottom near Kilnsey, and in Cove Hole near Grassington.

Jubilee Cave to Settle

Walk down to go over wall-stile and on over the moor to woodside track-way and follow it down to the roadway to go through gate on left. Follow path on along the brow of the hill to go through gate in wall between trees. Follow path on, through wall-gate and on to go over wall-stile by gate. Follow wallside trackway on to enter walled track that leads you down to Settle.

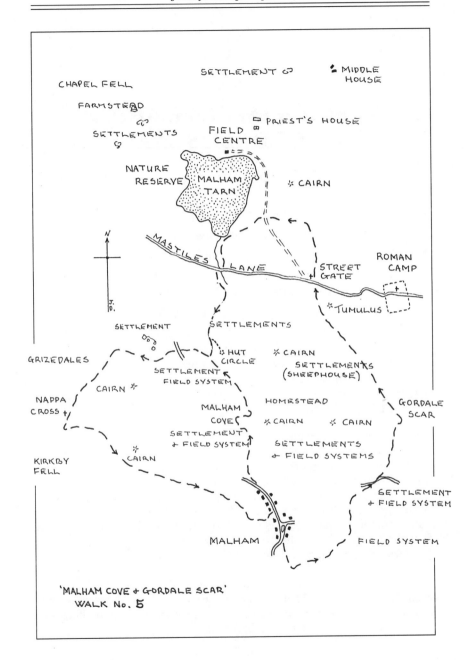

'MALHAM COVE & GORDALE SCAR'
WALK No. 5

Walk 5

MALHAM COVE AND GORDALE SCAR

6½ & 4½ miles, 3 to 4 hours & 2 to 3 hours.
Packed Lunch.

MAP:	*O.S. OUTDOOR LEISURE 10.*
	Yorkshire Dales, Southern Area.
START:	*Sparth House Hotel, Malham.*
ROUTE 1:	*Malham, Gordale Scar, Malham Tarn and Malham Cove.*
ROUTE 2:	*Malham, Malham Cove, Nappa Cross.*

October and March are good months for an exploration of Malham, being relatively free of tourists, who tend to get under the feet. If you do visit in summer use a none-holiday weekday. On my visits here in the long summer months I tend to use the very early morning and evening for my pleasure, thus avoiding the 'wandering horde'.

Malham and the surrounding area is surely a great wonder of Nature. The monstrous chasm of Gordale with its rushing cataracts and hanging walls brings a threatening shudder to spectators upon first viewing. In contrast the Tarn is a tranquil idyll of clear blue water reflecting the wooded scar-backdrop on its mirror-like surface. Such a setting brought forth Kingsley's "Water Babies", and led Ruskin to ponder. Where torrents once rushed people now walk down the dry valley to the head of that ancient waterfall that once roared forth down to the foot of the Cove. The views all round from the limestone pavement are deep, long and magnificent.

Malham itself is a lovely village blessed with all the visitor could require: good shops, fine inns and hotels, tea rooms galore, gift/craft shops, an outdoor shop and a great information centre. And, surprisingly enough, nothing is on the expensive side. An arcadia within Arcadia.

Malham Village

The village site goes back to the 8th century, but what we see today belongs to the 17th & 18th centuries. In the 1086 Norman Survey the village is named 'Malgun', said to mean *"the place of Malcas' clan"*.

The village economy was based on sheep farming, cattle grazing, some local spinning and weaving, and the mining of lead, copper, calamine and ore of zinc.

Malham Hall stood where the Reading Room now is, this was once the home of the steward of one moiety of the manor. The steward of the other moiety lived at the 'Old Hall', now Beck Hall.

Many houses display chamfered stone mullioned windows, and a few have datestones: Hill Top Farm, with a gabled porch, has a datestone of 1617. The single-storey Old Grammar School is dated 1682, and the Lister Arms, once known as Dixon's, has an oval panel over the doorway with the date 1723.

Town Head, on the west side of the cove road, stands on the site of the old Calamine House, a warehouse for the finished product of the Smelt Mill below the Tarn. The calamine was taken to the canal wharf at Gargrave by pack-horse, then barged to Skipton to be used in the brass industry.

My favourite watering hole in the village is the Buck Inn - it caters for walkers and serves excellent food and ale at very reasonable prices. The mosaic on the floor was a gift of John Ruskin. Ruskin was a friend of Walter Morrison of Tarn House.

ROUTE 1

Malham to Janet's Foss

Cross the footbridge opposite Sparth House Hotel and follow track to the right, over three stiles and on to the left passing field barn to go over stile to enter Janet's Foss Wood (notice barn on left dated I.H. 1755 on doorhead). Walk on to the waterfall.

Janet's Fosse

Janet is the name of a local fairy queen, and is said to inhabit the small cave behind the apron of the foss (Old Norse for waterfall). Another cave lies across the stream under a delightful little curved fold in the limestone. Beside the pool is a walled sheep-wash fold. Prior to clipping, sheep were washed here as clean wool was more of value than a dirty, greasy fleece. On a warm summer's day the pool with its tumbling waters is an inviting place indeed.

Janet's Foss to Gordale Scar

Follow path to road, right and walk on, over Gordale Bridge and on to enter Gordale Scar trackway via gate on left. Follow track to waterfall.

Gordale Scar

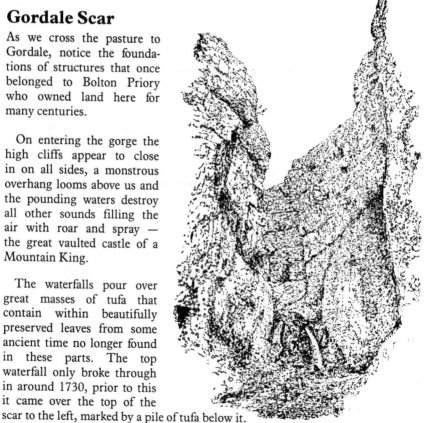

As we cross the pasture to Gordale, notice the foundations of structures that once belonged to Bolton Priory who owned land here for many centuries.

On entering the gorge the high cliffs appear to close in on all sides, a monstrous overhang looms above us and the pounding waters destroy all other sounds filling the air with roar and spray — the great vaulted castle of a Mountain King.

The waterfalls pour over great masses of tufa that contain within beautifully preserved leaves from some ancient time no longer found in these parts. The top waterfall only broke through in around 1730, prior to this it came over the top of the scar to the left, marked by a pile of tufa below it.

Above the falls is the Scar itself, a mile-long deep trench cut through the limestone plateau with almost vertical limestone cliffs throughout its length. The finest example of a limestone gorge that can be seen.

Gordale Scar is due to the presence of the Craven Fault and is its principle feature, caused by the work of streams eroding through long ages. Before the last Ice Age, Gordale Scar was a great cavern, the roof of which subsequently collapsed. A small fault crosses the scar between the two waterfalls forming a cave on the east side of the water above the lower fall. Here the displacement of the limestone is clearly recognisable.

The Craven Fault is a long fracture in the rocks of the earth's crust. Considerable vertical movement of the rocks either side of the fracture relative to one another has brought forth the formations we see today, like cutting a layered cake in half and raising one half against the side of the other exposing the layered section.

Stridebut Edge Iron Age Settlement
SD 907638

At Stridebut Edge we find a complete Iron Age settlement comprising several enclosures and hutments with associated field systems. The most intriguing feature of this site are the 'hollow walls' of which nine examples are known on the moor. A number of these wall passages have been cleared out and left open to view.

All are associated with enclosures in one wall of which, much broader than the others, a central trench type passage has been formed by careful building. This passage is between 2 to 3ft wide and around 2ft deep. The passage is usually between 30 to 40ft long, with one end opening into the enclosure and the other blocked by boulders or natural rock.

Their purpose is unknown and they remain an enigma for the present. Other such constructions have been located in the wider Dales, yet only in limestone areas.

Gordale Scar to Street Gate

Climb up the waterfall (very easy) and on up past the spout to the stile above the Scar. Good views over to the right. Pass over stile and follow path through the limestone avenue, passing cairns to go over wall-stile onto road. Follow wallside trackway to Street Gate.

Prior Rake Sheephouse
SD 905648

In the Compotus of Bolton Priory, and in subsequent years, account is taken of timber sent to Malham for repair of their Sheephouse there. The Sheephouse was manned by a shepherd and four foldmen who looked after the 2,000 sheep there (1300). The Sheephouse supplied the Priory with ewe milk cheese and butter, as well as wool and meat.

The site is located in a broad grassy valley at Prior Rake and consists of a very large enclosure and several smaller ones. The large one is rectangular, 48ft by 18ft inside with wall foundations 4ft wide and 18ins high, built with large boulders on edge on the two faces, filled with a packing of smaller stones, with a well finished and level top. On this would have rested the timber framed Sheephouse. Near it stands another rectangular building, 20ft by 15ft, with a hearth built in one corner. Adjoining this there is a walled enclosure some 20ft wide with regular set, deep post holes down the wall centre. Artifacts found on the site belonged to the 14th century.

The Sheephouse would have been used for wintering the breeding ewes, and the shepherd would have resided here also. The other smaller building would have housed the four foldmen, the other building would have been sheds and lean-to structures.

Seaty Hill Tumulus

On the approach to Street Gate we notice over the right the rise of Seaty Hill with its burial mound atop. The top is surrounded by a shallow ditch and low bank, enclosing a low mound 66ft in diameter. The mound upon excavation was seen to cover a seated skeleton burial made in a hole cut in the top of the hill, with another hole alongside with a stone cairn in it. The whole had been covered with a gravel mound. A typical Bronze Age burial of c.1800 B.C.

Sometime in the 1st century B.C. the Iron Age Brigantes had interred a further thirteen persons in the top of the mound in shallow bowl-shaped graves. Here, among the bone fragments, there were found iron knives, a few beads, and in a central grave, a small bone flute with three finger holes.

Street Gate to Malham Tarn

Follow trackway directly on over and down to cattle grid (do not go over) and follow left-hand wall, then fence to Trackway. Walk directly on, passing wall corner on down to Tarn Foot.

Malham Tarn

The Tarn is a natural lake lying on a floor of impervious Silurian slate that has been brought near the surface by the North Craven Fault. The waters are confined by a glacial moraine, a long train of heaps of clay and gravel deposited by the retreating ice at the end of the last Ice Age. A good section of moraine can be seen in gravel pits on the way up from Street Gate. The wooded slopes of Highfolds Scar provide an enchanting backdrop to the clear blue waters.

Tarn House was built by Walter Morrison to replace an earlier hunting lodge of the Listers, Lords Ribblesdale. It was whilst staying at Tarn House, on a visit to the Malham district, that Charles Kingsley gained much inspiration for his book, "The Water Babies". And who could not fail to gain creative thought from such a setting. The house is now a Field Studies Centre for all manner of research into the surrounding area.

Above Highfold Scar are a number of archaeological sites that are worth a mention here:

Priest's House, Highfold Scar
SD 897674

Above Malham Tarn, on the edge of Great Close, can be found a large stone rectangular house, 15ft by 9ft inside, with two slender partition walls. Excavation of the house site produced 7th century artifacts that included a finely made bronze brooch with a gold inlay in the Celtic style, book edging and strap ends of bronze and small buckles. The site here represents a Celtic Monastic cell, the abode of a member of the British clergy.

In the Life of Wilfrid by Eddius Stephanus we read that taking over the Bishopric of York, Wilfrid was granted land "round Ribble, Yeadon, Dent and Catlow, and in other places too." From these holy places had fled the British clergy from the hostile Anglian sword leaving them deserted.

It is now strongly suspected that the Celtic Church in some of its forms survived the c.678 onslaught, especially west of the Pennines. Ecclesiastical customs at Whalley in Blackburnshire, the site of the 7th century monastery of Paegnalaech, at the time of the Conquest are seen to be Celtic in nature owing little to the Roman Church.

It is possible that the Malham cell also survived Wilfrid's onslaught.

Mediaeval Farm, Highfold Scar
SD 897675

Just above the Priest's House site can be found the remains of a Mediaeval farm. All that remain are the stone foundations of a timber-framed building, 25ft by 13ft inside, with one end rounded. Around one third of the floor area was paved with small flaggy stones, and the rest was of pounded loam. The building had a hearth and the doorway was near the rounded end. A whetstone and fragments of 11th and 12th century pottery were found during the excavation of the building.

In the 12th century, Fountains Abbey was granted Malham Moor and its sheep farms, yet this site and five other similar farm sites are not accounted for in the Abbey records. It would seem that the Highfold Scar site, along with the others, are the remains of earlier economic activity in the area which were abandoned when Fountains took over the management of the Moor.

Middle House Iron Age Village
SD 901681

Upon a limestone promontary at Middle House Pasture is an Iron Age village site enclosed by a well defined wall. The village consists of nineteen buildings. Eight circular dwelling houses between 25ft to 35ft in diameter, free-standing with walls 3 to 4 feet thick. Around the three sides of this hut group is a wall into which, or against which, have been built another 13 huts slightly smaller in size, these are grouped in twos and threes.

Upon excavation of one hut it was seen to have been built on a strong, low foundation wall with post holes for fairly close set vertical posts that would have supported the roof. The floor was made of compacted marl and there was a hearth with an amount of charcoal. Pottery and a glass bead from the site placed the whole into an Iron Age setting. Some of the smaller grouped huts are thought to have been granaries. The surrounding village wall was constructed of large boulders and is 1,300 ft in length.

The village has, for some distance around it, many isolated hut circles of the period that would have had economic and social connections with it.

Having a surrounding wall, these sites are often referred to as 'defended village sites'. This is a misnomer, as it suggests military defence, whereas the wall should be seen as a territorial boundary, on a modern day par to the farmyard wall or your garden fence or hedge.

Chapel Fell Settlements
SD 881672

The settlement on Castle Fell consists of several interconnected enclosures with two circular huts. Just outside the main enclosure, built across an old bank is a rectangular building 12ft by 26ft inside, divided into a large and small room. Another rectangular building, 9½ft by 19½ft inside, is located in one of the smaller enclosures cutting into its walls, again divided into a large and small room.

In the circular huts, several sherds of native pottery were found. The rectangular buildings produced sherds of 3rd century pottery and remains of three quern stones, one being a complete bottom stone set on a well constructed pedestal of large stones. The broken top stone lay close by. In one of the enclosures, slag and iron fragments with charcoal mark the site of a forge. There are no field systems around the site, only a number of animal folds.

Here we have a native Iron Age site with later buildings being erected during the Roman period, displaying the contact that would have existed between Brigantian tribesmen and Roman soldiers and their mutual economic bond.

Just to the north of the above site, at SD 883676, is the site of a building some 90ft by 45ft in size. When excavated the walls remained in parts about three feet high, well built on good footings. A section of flooring is paved at the east end, the rest being cobbled. The only door is at the south west corner, well framed with two steps. The roof had been tiled with Silurian slate that may have come from the Austwick quarries, one of the properties of Fountains Abbey.

Given the type of walling and lack of wall debris, one may assume it to have been a stone building with a slate roof that had been used as a quarry when it fell into disuse. The property would have belonged to the abbey at Fountains.

Tradition holds that the Abbey once had a chapel near the tarn, and the above site is thought to be this building.

Near the 'Chapel' site are a number of round hut sites that vary between 20 to 30 feet in diameter. Finds from the site include numerous worked flints and several stone axes. Excavation proved the huts to have been constructed of timber, based on gravel banks round a shallow bowl-shaped hollow. A

Neolithic date is placed on these structures, and the whole, some nine dwellings, must be seen as a single hunting community with pastoral input.

It was these people who first started to clear the great forest that would have covered the district then, elm, alder, oak and lime being most common then, having replaced the earlier hazel and pine in dominance and growing at heights, possibly 1,500 feet above sea level. The Grass Wood site at Grassington gives us a good picture of what the landscape would have been like in those times — limestone scars hidden by trees.

Tarn Foot to Malham Cove

Follow path down to roadway, right and cross raised ford to go through gate over on the left (notice Smelt Mill chimney over on right). Walk on to follow left-hand pathway, past the water sink, and on to enter limestone gorge (if you wish to visit Comb Hill Hut Circle then work your way up the opposite side of the gorge and walk over to the right for some way to above a valley where you will view the circle below). Follow the path on and down into Ing Scar dry valley and on to the top of the Cove. Caution: in wet conditions the limestone pavement above the Cove can be very slippery. Take care.

The Smelt Mill Chimney

The chimney occupies a prominent position to the south of the ruined Smelt Mill. The mill served the lead mines on Pikedaw and Langscar. Little remains of the mill now, only the wall foundations and part of the flue from the smelting hearth. Traces of the dam and washing floors exist but are difficult to recognise.

Comb Hill Hut Circle

In the well sheltered valley below Comb Hill is the excavated, preserved remains of a Bronze Age house. The dwelling is circular, 19ft diameter inside thick boulder walls five to six feet thick and now about two feet high. At the centre of the hut is a deep post hole that once held the main roof-post. Fragments of Bronze Age pottery and small worked flints were found during the excavation. The site provides us with a valuable resource in our understanding of Bronze Age life.

Sheriff Hill Round Cairn

Above the Cove, to the east on Sheriff Hill, can be found a round cairn burial mound. This prominent structure stands amid ancient Celtic fields and is almost 100 feet in diameter. The mound was originally constructed in the Bronze Age proved by the finds of sherds of an Incense Cup, a Collared Urn and a possible Food Vessel. As with Seaty Hill, later Iron Age burials took place here.

When the mound was first dug into in c.1845, along with many human bones of secondary burial, fragments of an iron spearhead were found. The site was then known as 'Friars Heap', and the burial then thought to be connected with the 'marauding Scots'. The cairn is possibly contemporary with the Comb Hill hut circle.

Malham Cove

The Cove is a curved crag of limestone, almost 300ft high at its centre, forming a bow with its ends three hundred yards apart. In past geological periods the Cove was a waterfall, nearly twice the height of Niagara, made by an ancient stream falling over the edge of a scarp caused by the Craven Fault. The summit of the Cove is occupied by fissured limestone pavement, 'clints'.

The clints provide a micro environment for many rare plants. A little look down will reveal woodsorrel, rue, aspleniums, enchanter's nightshade and geranium to name but a few. Do not be tempted to pull them out, they will never grow in your garden and you take away the joy of others and bring upon yourself bad karma.

At the foot of the Cove a stream emerges from under the rock. This stream starts to the north west of the Smelt Mill and disappears by the Smelt Mill Watersinks to appear again below the Cove as Malham Beck. The waters of

Malham Tarn disappear below the roadway at the Tarn Watersinks to emerge at Airehead Springs.

Above the Cove is the Dry Valley, a long limestone channel that once brought the water to the magnificent waterfall. During periods of torrential downpours the waters have been known to once again tumble over the Cove, falling in a veil of spray. Such a site would be a great joy and pleasure to see.

The views from above the Cove are vast and deep. We see beyond Craven into the Trawden Forest with the bulk of Boulsworth as a backdrop. To the right the Lion of Pendle rests above the Ribble Valley, and to the left Rylstone Fell guards the Aire Gap and the Central Pennine region. Below us we can make out the raised outline of Celtic (Iron Age/Romano-British) field boundaries amid the later 16th century divisions.

From the top of the Cove a footpath leads eastward to the important burial mound on Sheriff Hill.

Malham Cove to Malham

Walk on over the limestone pavement and follow the path down to the foot of the Cove and on to the roadway above the village. Walk down into the village and the Buck Inn.

ROUTE 2

Malham to Malham Cove

Walk up through the village to leave the roadway by stile on right and follow the footpath on to the foot of the Cove. Follow the path up to the left to the top of the Cove.

Malham Cove to Langscar Settlement

Follow the path on through Ings Scar dry valley to go up the rocky steps and over a stile. Follow wall on to go over wall-stile on left. Walk directly on to go over stile onto road. Pass through the gate opposite and follow the trackway on (glance over wall on right after some way to view settlement) to gateway.

Langscar Iron Age Village

Up on the grassy slopes of Langscar there is a very large group of Iron Age hutments and fields. The enclosures are mainly rectangular and separated from one another by turf and gravel banks set with large stones. It is among these fields that the hut circles are to be found, often backed up against the low rock scars. The huts take the form of circular banks enclosing an area of about 10ft diameter. The site has yielded fragments of pottery and other artifacts that establish the site to an Iron Age date. The people who lived in this village would have kept goats and sheep, and made use of the wild cattle. Horse breeding would also have taken place. Tools connected with weaving and animal skinning were found in small numbers within the camp area.

Langscar Settlement to Nappa Cross

Pass through the gateway and walk up the hill to the left to pass through gateway and follow track on to go through next two gateways and on up to Nappa cross that is set on top of a field wall.

Nappa Cross

Nappa Cross is set on top of a field wall at the summit of the bridleway over Pikedaw to Stockdale and Settle, at a point where the path from Malham Tarn and Langscar join it. It consists of the base of a wayside cross with a short section of the shaft set into the socket hole. The cross originally stood close to its present position at the junction of the bridleways, and was just a plain shaft with no cross arm. It dates from the monastic period, being around 550 years old, one of many that are located on the moorland trackways. Another cross lies in the wall at Weets top, at the junction of Hanlith, Bordley and Calton Moors, again on an ancient bridleway.

From Nappa Cross a very fine view is to be obtained of Malham Tarn and the surrounding moors of Rylstone, Skipton and Bowland.

Nappa Cross to Malham

Follow wall on to go through gate on left. Follow track down to signpost and follow the path to the right on and then down (notice the gritstone scar over on the right) to go over wall-stile. Follow path on down, over stile by gate and on down to go over stile by barn. Follow path on to cross stream at wall and on to go over wall-stile onto farm lane. Left, then right to follow lane on down to Malham.

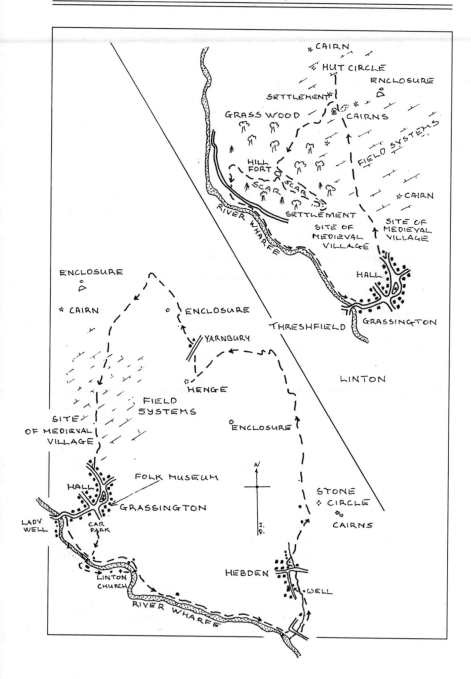

Walk 6

STONE CIRCLES AND LOST VILLAGES

GRASSINGTON/HEBDEN WALK — 9 miles, 5 hours.

GRASS WOOD WALK — 5½ miles, 3 hours.

LUNCH: *Clarendon Hotel, Hebden. Foresters Arms, Grassington.*

MAP: *O.S. OUTDOOR LEISURE 10, Yorkshire Dales, Southern Area.*

START: *The National Park Car Park, Grassington, or Hebden Village.*

Today Grassington is a busy tourist and commuter village set within superb landscape that reflects the ancient and modern Dales economy. On Grassington Moor old lead mines and workings dominate the hillsides and valleys, worked for nearly 2,000 years. Over to the west, Swinden quarry still extracts limestone, an eyesore to many, but a vital industry all the same.

Tourism is hailed as the 'new industry', but I have strong doubts. One can only hope that the products for sale in local shops reflect local craft industries and trades and not the general mass produced tourist paraphernalia that can be found anywhere. The problem is one of balance between the traditional rural economy and the new exploitation of the landscape by tourism.

This walk is designed to explore and gain a fuller appreciation of this delightful area. The two ancient circular monuments viewed on today's visit are amongst the most important in the Southern Dales and will not disappoint.

One can get down to the river either by a walled pathway that is entered by a gate in the southern corner of the car park area. The pathway comes out at Tin Bridge, Linton Falls.

Or one can follow the following directions:

National Park Car Park to River Bridge
Walk out of the car park and follow the road round to the left to the Wharfe bridge. Follow path down to the riverbank.

Linton Bridge & Lady Well Cottage
Close examination of the bridge stonework will reveal traces of the old pack-horse, humpbacked bridge of 1603. Notice the two stages of building under the arches and the masons marks.

On the opposite bank of the river is Lady Well Cottage. The house has an original 16th century cruck-frame construction within its 17th century exterior of mullioned windows.

South of the cottage, sited upon common land, is the Lady Well, and just beyond the 17th century houses of Bridge End and Gams Bank. The latter is dated 1631 with the initials S.M.

Linton Bridge to Linton Parish Church
Follow the riverside pathway on to Tin Bridge above Linton Falls, created by the North Craven Fault. (The weir and ruined building that we passed on our way to the bridge was once part of an old hydro-electric station. Also notice the Jacobean barn to the left of the bridge. A stone on the west wall bears a date of 1682, with the initials H.W. The two doorheads are also of interest.) Cross over Tin Bridge and follow the path round to the road and follow it on to the church.

The Old Threshfield and Linton Mills etc
'Tin Bridge' refers to the original bridge across Linton Falls that was built for the workers at Linton Mill in 1914. The flooring was then covered with tin sheets formed from old oil drums. Today's bridge is the fourth to be erected across the falls. Built of timber, it was opened in 1989.

Once across the bridge take a peep over the wall on the left. Here the mechanism for opening the Old Mill sluice gate stands intact as a now garden feature. The 1790 water-powered mill of the Birkbeck's has all but been demolished to be replaced by new residential housing. In its day, the mill was five storeys in height and spun woollen yarns.

As we follow the path round, an old packhorse bridge appears over on the left. This is known as Little Emily's Bridge said to be named after Emily Norton who took refuge hereabouts at the time of the Civil War. The bridge was constructed in monastic times like so many others throughout the Dales.

A pathway over the bridge leads to Threshfield Mill, the left-hand of the three cottages. This once corn mill dates from the 17th century and was powered by a small leet taken from Captain Beck. It operated until the late 19th century and later became a creamery.

LINTON CHURCH.

Linton Church

Before entering the churchyard, look over in the field on the right. The large standing-stone sited there is said to mark a pre-Christian religious site.

The Church of St. Michael and All Angels serves the villages of Linton, Grassington, Threshfield and, previously, Hebden. A dedication to St. Michael suggests an early 10th century Scandinavian origin for the church, he being popular with the Christian Vikings by being near in type to their old Nordic gods.

The oldest parts of the edifice date from the Norman period, being the robust circular font and the two east bays of the north arcade. The inposts of the chancel arch are also Norman. The windows are a mix of Decorated 14th century, and Perpendicular 15th century styles, all very delightful.

In the south wall of the nave are two tomb recesses and there is another in the north wall, alas with no monuments. Other tombs and memorial brasses in the church date from the 17th century and onwards and are of little interest. Notice the pre-Reformation stone altar.

The rarest and most important possession of the church was an 11th century Romanesque crucifix. I say was, because sadly this relic was stolen by antique dealers some years ago. The crucifix was found in 1835 near one of the fords over the stream at Linton when one of the Dean family of Manor House farm was building a new barn near the present almshouses.

Even given the shocking theft, Linton Church is always open to the public — a refreshing display of true Christian trust. A very good guide book to this squat belfried gem of a church is available at a small cost inside the church — well worth a read.

During the Spring months, on the river walk between Linton and Hebden, look out for Birds Eye Primrose and Butterwort.

Linton Church to Hebden Bridge

If the river is low then we can cross the Wharfe by way of the hipping stones that lie to the east of the churchyard and follow the path on to Hebden suspension bridge. Otherwise we must retrace our footsteps back to go across Tin Bridge and follow the riverside pathway on to go over a wall-stile over on the left onto farm lane. Follow lane down past the fish farm to go over stile by gate. Follow the riverside pathway on down to Hebden suspension bridge.

Hebden Suspension Bridge

The bridge was built by the Hebden village blacksmith, William Bell, in 1985. It replaces the old and worn hipping-stones that stand just down river.

When we walk up the little valley to Hebden, notice the weir, waterfall, Thruskell 'holy' Well, old mill race and other remains of former village industry now overgrown by natural vegetation.

Hebden Bridge to Clarendon Hotel, Hebden

Pass through wall-gate and walk up to the right to go through wall-gate onto roadway. Right, and walk on over the bridge to follow path on left, between houses and on through gates to go over footbridge. Follow path on and up to the roadway by the village school. Right, and follow roadway on to junction above bridge. The pub is up on the left.

Hebden

Hebden was once a busy mining village and its architecture owes much to that period with a number of the buildings dating from the 17th century. Our walk from Hebden up to Yarnbury Henge is a haven for industrial archaeologists being once the most intensively mined area of Wharfedale. Horizontal levels and vertical shafts, driven to tap the rich lead veins, are abundant in and on the moors around Hebden Gill. These shafts, though partly concealed, are open and EXTREMELY DANGEROUS.

The informed will pick out washing floors and ore crushing mills among the many spoil heaps. The recently restored smelt mill chimney is highly prominent on the eastern hillside but little now remains of the complex system of aqueducts and waterwheels that once made up this vast enterprise.

The valley in its heyday would have been an unwelcoming place, but Nature, in her wisdom, with help from Father Time, has done much to transform the worst of the dereliction and the dark gritstone boulders and crags that stand sentinel above the gill appeal to all lovers of ruinous grandeur.

Please keep small and inquisitive children near to hand till we reach Yarnbury Henge. If you wish to learn more about lead mining in the area may I suggest a visit to the Earby Mines Museum, Earby and the Craven Museum, Skipton.

Clarendon Hotel to Dumpit Stone Circle

Walk down the lane on the left of the road bridge and over old bridge to go between buildings on right, then up to the left to go over wall-stile at footpath sign (Scar Top). Follow path up to the left (notice 17th century windows at rear of houses) to go over wall-stile.

Walk up the field to go over wall-stile, then over to the left to go over next wall-stile. Follow path on up through the bracken to go over wall-stile and walk on to go over next wall-stile. Continue on up to go over wall-stile and on up past Scar Side House to leave the lane after a short way to follow wallside trackway on left up to go over wall-stile on left.

Walk up the moor onto trackway and follow it to the left to Scar Top cattle grid. Right, and walk out onto the moor to the Stone Circle, marked by a large upright stone.

Dumpit Stone Circle

The Stone Circle stands to the east of the 17th century upland farmstead of Scar Top House. Views from the moor top are splendid: Simon's Seat atop of

Barden Fell and Burnsall and Thorpe Fell stand aside the wide valley of the Wharfe above Bolton Priory. Over to the far south-west Longridge and Bowland fells can be made out, even Parlick Pike comes into view.

Much controversy exists as to the function of such stone circles with theories ranging from ancient temples to agrarian calendars. However, it is now thought that such complexes represent contemporary sites for ritual and burial respectively, yet even this theory can only explain a part of their role and function. More co-operation between disciplines is needed to understand their true nature and a starting point must be the first permanent settlements in the area.

Stone Circle to Yarnbury Henge

Walk back to wall at cattlegrid and follow the wallside trackway on to go through gate and on to go through next gate. Walk on over the moor to go through gate and on to go through next two gates. Follow path down (notice old mine level up the clough on the right) to ford main stream onto trackway and through gate to follow trackway on upstream, then up and round to the left to go through gate on right at Bridleway sign.

Follow track on to go through gateway and on to junction. Left, and walk on to around the bend to leave the track and walk down to the left past walls to go through wall-stile and across field to go through next wall-stile. Continue on to go through gateway and on to go through wall-stile. The Henge is over on the left.

Yarnbury Henge

Yarnbury Henge is a large circular earthwork of about 100ft. diameter, crest to crest of the bank, and in the inner part about 70ft. in diameter, a raised vallum and inner ditched disc barrow of Bronze Age origin.

Disc barrows have a deep ditch sometimes, as here, with an external bank (Vallum). The central mound is reduced to very small proportions, and in some cases, scarcely visible. Instead of tools and weapons, these usually contain jewellery, ornaments, sewing implements and domestic pottery, and it has been assumed that they are the graves of important women.

The views from the Henge are magnificent, and notice how the great Lion of Pendle dominates the far skyline. In the winter months the sun falls behind Pendle providing it with a sky-red backdrop. In my own view the site is related to the presence of Pendle, itself a Bronze Age ritual site, and may have been the major factor in the location of the monument.

Whilst in the area of Yarnbury, look out for the Mountain Pansy, common here and around Victoria Cave, above Settle, in the Springtime.

Grassington Field Systems

On our way down to the village from Yarnbury we shall pass through an area of Romano-British and later, early mediaeval field systems. The former consist of a network of stone and turf banks, dividing the area into a large number of approximately oblong fields lying roughly north-east to south-west.

Amid these fields are several hut circles and burial mounds (see enlarged map of area in 'Grass Wood' walk), some related to the fields and others from earlier periods (see Lea Green walk). The Mediaeval field systems take the form of cultivation terraces, lynchets, and even these may have been established in the earlier Celtic period.

Yarnbury Henge to Grassington

Go back through the wall-stile and gate, then cross the field heading up to the left to go through wall-stile onto lane at Yarnbury (once a busy mining settlement, now only a house and weekend cottage). Right, and walk on to go up drive on left to follow path on to the right to reach wallside trackway. Left, and walk up to the corner. (The enclosure is in the next field but one in front of you.)

Continue on along the trackway (notice the walls: limestone on the left, gritstones, with a boulder base, on the right), over the rise and through gateway. Follow left-hand wall on to go over wall below perched limestone boulders. Walk on and head down to the right to go over wall-stile. Walk on to go over wall-stile over on the left. Continue on same line to go through wall-gate. Follow the waymarked path down over the field systems, via stiles, to Grassington village.

Roman Lead Mines, Grassington

Lead has been mined in this region of Yorkshire since before Roman times. From the Roman period we have smelted lead pigs which carry the names of the Emperors Domitian, Trajan and Hadrian (81-138 A.D.) indicating a well established and organised industry around Swaledale and Wharfedale.

A lead pig weighing 156 pounds was found in the area of Hagshaw Bank in 1735. It bears the official Roman mark of Domitian, 81 A.D., with the word 'BRIG', showing that it came from the province of Brigantia. Traces of this Brigantian mining activity can be found on Greenhow Hill, Grassington.

In the 12th century the Cistercian houses of Byland, Fountains and Jervaulx and the Augustinian Priories of Bolton and Bridlington were granted rights to mine iron and lead in the Dales. The final smelted product was used in the construction of religious houses both in Britain and on the continent.

After the Dissolution, these mining areas came into secular ownership and a phase of intensive exploitation began that only ended in recent times.

GRASSINGTON — GRASS WOOD WALK

This walk takes us through an area of extensive ancient settlement and we refer you to the larger Lea Green map for navigating your way to and around the sites.

Grassington National Park Centre to Mediaeval Village Site

Walk up Main Street to go right at the Town Hall along Chapel Street and through Town Head and on to enter farmyard at 'Conistone' footpath sign. Walk on to bear left between barns to come out onto field trackway. Follow right-hand 'Conistone' footpath to go through middle gate. We now walk through an area on which stood the mediaeval village of Grassington, and earlier Romano-British settlements.

Mediaeval Village Sites

To the west of Bank Lane are two areas of large settlement, that for a lack of investigation and the want of a precise nature have been described as 'mediaeval'. The sites consist of huts, enclosures and tracks discernable in their outline by mounds of stone and earth. Given the number of Bronze/Iron Age sites in the area one can fairly assume that settlement took firm root here in those times. It would also be fair to assume that this settlement was continuous right up to the Norman Conquest.

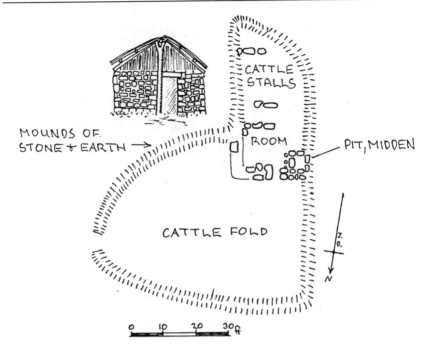

MOUNDS OF. STONE + EARTH →

CATTLE STALLS

ROOM

PIT, MIDDEN

CATTLE FOLD

0   10   20   30 ft

MEDIAEVAL DWELLING, LEA GREEN.
(NORTH END OF LEA GREEN PASTURE)

What is referred to as a rectangular Iron Age or Romano-British hut and enclosure site, could just as easily be referred to as a Viking or Norse hut and enclosure site, as the building techniques are the same. An enlightened mind would see our Scandinavian settler utilizing the same structure and farm sites as those who worked the land before him.

For example: a hut and enclosure at the north end of Lea Green Pasture is seen by one authority as a Celtic homestead, and by another as a summer far-pasture cow shed of the 9th/10th century (see diagram); neither consider continuity of settlement in their analysis.

The village sites at Grassington represent a thousand years plus settlement up to a time somewhat after the Norman Conquest when, for some reason, the old village was abandoned and a new one established on the site of today's village. Plague or the 'Harrying of the North' could have brought this about.

DMV Site to Lea Green Homestead

From the middle gate, walk directly on to go through wall-stile. Follow path on and around to the top left to go through wall-stile and on to go over wall-stile. Follow path directly on and over Lea Green, and down to an area of raised limestone pavement on the right with a few scant trees growing upon it.

Walk on for twenty yards to come upon the Iron Age settlement. Stop amongst the rocks, look over to the left and train your eyes to look for low-walled rectangular hutments within the limestone. See Lea Green enlarged map to gain full value from the site.

Lea Green Burial Mounds

There are many burial sites on and around Lea Green, here I shall limit the study to just four of the barrows.

To the east of Bank Lane (see plan: M1), amid the Borrans field system is a Bronze Age Tumulus, that when excavated yielded an all-over decorated beaker, 7ins. high, along with a crouched skeleton burial. Along with the beaker, now restored and on display in Craven Museum, was found a small piece of polished green stone that has been described as impure "jade". Another Bronze Age burial on Lea Green yielded a food vessel.

To the north of the above site is a multiple burial barrow (M2) 62 feet in diameter and between 1 and 3 feet high. It is circular and constructed of boulders, gravel and earth.

In the centre of the barrow was found a rectangular grave 7ft. by 3ft. with a skeleton buried 4ft. below the mound surface. The body was doubled up with the legs up to the chin and the head facing east. Near the body was an iron knife hafted in deer bone and a piece of worked bone.

Four other burials were found in the mound along with numerous animal bones: ox, sheep, goat, stag, wild boar, fox, dog and rat. A bronze ring, a knife handle, a bone pin and a flat jet button were also found. The mound is of Iron Age origin.

At the centre of Lea Green is a slightly oval barrow (M3), 76ft. east to west, and 66ft. north to south. It contained seven burials in various locations within the mound, and associated with them were four iron knives, a bronze pin, a bronze razor and a bone pin.

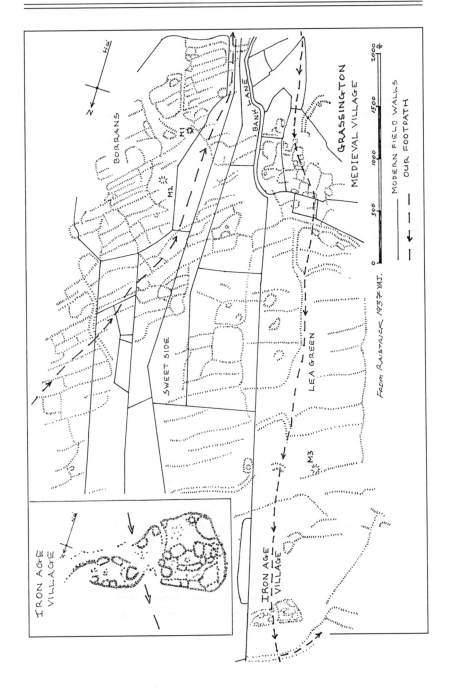

Iron Age Village Site

Located at the north end of Lea Green are a number of Iron Age settlements, the largest being the one we are now viewing, being a village site rather than a large farmstead. As the eye focuses in, one after another a great number of low-walled former buildings come into view, the whole being enclosed within a larger system of low walls.

Archaeological excavations on the site have revealed artifacts that extend from possibly second century B.C. to third century A.D. These include many types of pottery, iron knives and sickles, bone spoons and pins — some decorated with incised bands and circles, stone and lead spindle whorls, beehive quern stones and many other related objects. Indeed, with its associated field systems, an important Brigantian village in its time.

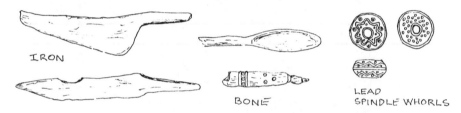

IRON

BONE

LEAD
SPINDLE WHORLS

On occasions when I have taken people around the Lea Green sites, we have never failed to find some ancient object or other. Our finds have been made by the inspection of mole heaps and careful field walking. The mole hills have yielded pottery and flint implements and our field walks have revealed enclosures and hutments so far unrecorded.

Looking over to the north east from the village site, one can pick out two ruined buildings abutting the walls of Sweet Side. It is worth making a diversion, via the wall-stile to the north, to view these two structures.

The northern building is known as Botton House and is a mediaeval house with most of its walls still standing to some height. It was described in 1605 as an 'ancient mansion house' belonging to the Earl of Cumberland. The southern house is sited near a spring which feeds into a system of watering troughs that are well worth viewing.

At the north end of Lea Green is a large tumulus, that when excavated revealed two circular walls with it. The outer one was 40ft. in diameter and the inner one eccentric to it and 16ft. in diameter.

(*FRAGMENTS OF*)
FOOD VESSEL

BEAKER

A grave pit was found in the centre of the inner circle, with a limestone slab cover and a skeleton on its right side, legs doubled up and facing west. A bone awl was found with this body. A number of other burials were found within the mound along with many animal bones.

In all the burials, apart from M1, there was no evidence of cremation rites and can be seen to have an Iron Age origin.

Lea Green
to Grass Wood Prehistoric Settlement Site

Follow path on to stone-lined avenue (line of old trackway) and follow it to the left, then around to the left to walk up to follow a trackway over to the right to go over wall-stile by gateway. Follow path up and on, through Bastow Wood to go over wall-stile into Grass Wood. Follow path on, left at the junction to go on down to the Prehistoric Settlement Site. (Ancient Monument sign).

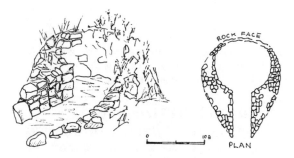

ROCK FACE

PLAN

Grass Wood Settlement Site

The rough section of hillside near Park Stile that we are now going to walk round is, as the Ancient Monument sign informs us, a prehistoric settle-

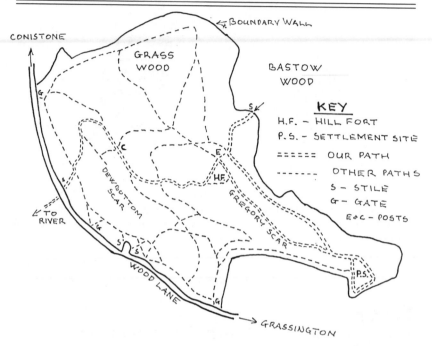

ment site, and affords us a fairly accurate picture of Bronze/Iron Age Dwellings. Here we find a number of circular Iron Age habitations and related earthworks.

The dwellings were dug out of the hillside to a depth of about 5ft., often backing onto a rock face that would provide a rear wall, then walls of coarse rubble were erected in a rough circle giving an interior diameter of about 10ft. The walls come round from 3 to 7 feet thick (see diagram). These tend to taper upwards leading one to think that they may have been stone 'bee hive' structures, with a central hearth, rather than thatched dwellings. A single passage served as an entrance, 3ft. wide and about 7ft. long.

Settlement Site to Fort Gregory

Follow path down to the left to wall-stile (DO NOT GO OVER). Follow path to the right, then up to the right back to the Settlement Site. Follow path back up to go left at fork and on along Gregory Scar, and on up to go down to the right below Far Gregory Hill Fort to post marked 'E'. Walk up to the left to the highest point of the hill fort, marked by a post 'FORT GREGORY AD 70'.

Far Gregory Iron Age Hill Fort

The stone fort of Far Gregory is situated within Grass Wood on an isolated limestone knoll, rising fairly abruptly in a series of limestone scars, 350ft. above the River Wharfe on the west and separated from the main plateau of the Lea Green settlements by a scarped depression of about 100ft.

The summit commands a superb view up and down the Wharfe and across the west for many miles. Against the stone wall are smaller enclosures, possible living huts. The edge of the scarp is emphasised and strengthened by the clearing of scree material and by rough, large boulder walling along the edge. Gullies and gaps in the scarp have been packed with rocks.

Outside the fort area the summit forms a walled enclosure about 500ft. by 200ft., which would have contained a great number of cattle and stock during times of hostilities for the people of the Lea Green settlements.

This Brigantian stronghold would have played a vital role in the defence of the Dales area of Brigantia during the Roman onslaught of 74 A.D. that led to the fall of Venutius, and the later occupation of the area that was to lead to the exploitation of the district's rich veins of lead.

Grass Wood

Grass Wood is sited upon a mass of Great Scar limestone which has south-west facing exposures on Dewbottom and Gregory Scars. The habitat is a fine example of ash and birch woodland on limestone with recent additions of mixed hardwoods and conifers. Selective felling is maintained to encourage the natural species of trees and attendant ground flora to become re-established. Look out for wild Lily of the Valley.

The ecological and historical importance of the wood is widely recognised. It gives us a living picture of the Dales before sheep farming destroyed the natural landscape.

Far Gregory to Grassington
via River Wharfe

From the Fort marker post at the summit follow path on and down, across a pathway and on and around to the right, right at junction and on to post marked 'C'. Follow path directly on, left as a path goes down, and on around to the left (here we gain a good view of the upper Wharfe and Kilnsey Crag)

*and on down to join lower pathway. Left, and walk on a few yards to go
down to the right onto roadway via stile. Pass over stile opposite and follow
riverside pathway down, over stiles, to Linton Bridge and on up the roadway
into Grassington.*

Grassington Old Hall

Grassington Old Hall is a wonderful survival from the 13th century, being one
of the oldest inhabited houses in the Yorkshire Dales. Part of the hall of the
later 13th century comprises two front windows on the first floor with tran-
soms and plate tracery (quartrefoil), a small twin lancet window at the rear of
the right wing, and an archway inside. Other windows are Tudor, and much
was altered in the late 19th century.

The Hall was built for Robert de Plumpton as a hunting lodge, and is said to
have once had a chapel.

Grassington

The village of Grassington deserves a book in itself. Most of the buildings date
from the 17th and 18th centuries and some incorporate the timber cruck
frames of earlier buildings.

As has been mentioned, the original settlement was at High Close, near
Grass Wood, the present town being established in the late 12th century when
the manor was transferred from the Percys to the Plumptons. In 1282 Grassington was granted a charter to hold a market and fair which became regular
features up to about 1860.

Well worth the outlay of 50p is "One Hundred Things to see on a Walk
through Grassington", by Ian Goldthorpe. It gives a short description and
history of almost every house in and around the village, all with excellent
illustrations. Available from booksellers in the village.

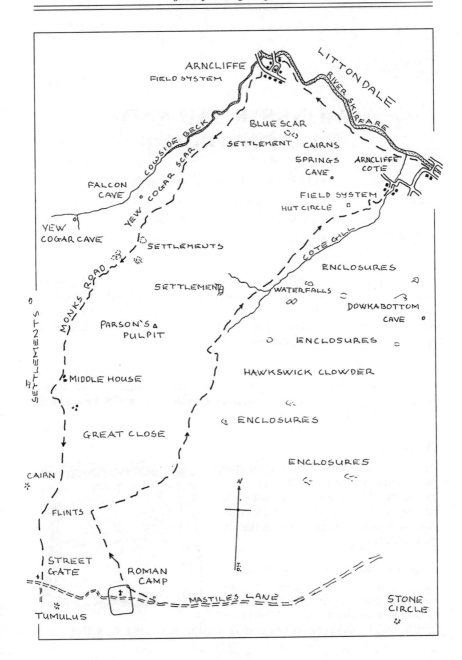

ARNCLIFFE
FIELD SYSTEM

LITTONDALE
RIVER SKIRFARE

COWSIDE BECK
YEW COGAR SCAR

BLUE SCAR
SETTLEMENT   CAIRNS
SPRINGS
CAVE

ARNCLIFFE
COTE

FALCON
CAVE

FIELD SYSTEM
HUT CIRCLE

YEW
COGAR CAVE

SETTLEMENTS

MONKS ROAD

SETTLEMENT

COTE GILL

ENCLOSURES

WATERFALLS

DOWKABOTTOM
CAVE

PARSON'S
PULPIT

ENCLOSURES

SETTLEMENTS

HAWKSWICK CLOWDER

MIDDLE HOUSE

ENCLOSURES

GREAT CLOSE

ENCLOSURES

CAIRN

N

FLINTS

STREET
GATE

ROMAN
CAMP

J.D.

MASTILES LANE

STONE
CIRCLE

TUMULUS

Walk 7

MONKS' ROAD AND PARSON'S PULPIT

11½ miles, 6 hours. Packed Lunch.

MAP: *O.S. OUTDOOR LEISURE 10,*
           Yorkshire Dales, Southern Area.

START: *Falcon Hotel, Arncliffe.*

On this walk we stride along the summit of that most dramatic of limestone scar formations, the Yew Cogar, best seen in all its glory from the Arncliffe to Malham road. Once atop we explore an area of ancient settlements of the Brigantes, then wander down through monastic farms and onto an archaic trackway to view a Roman Camp above Gordale Scar.

From here we gently climb up to below the Parson's Pulpit to find the cascading waters of Cote Gill Scar, and follow the troublesome rill down to the River Skirfare. Then a riverside walk leads us to the church of St Oswald and Arncliffe once again.

Arncliffe

Arncliffe stands at the foot of Littondale on the banks of the River Skirfare and is approached by an avenue of sycamores leading to the large village green criss-crossed by trackways that meet at the old stone water pump.

Around the green, stone cottages cluster, the small dwellings of the craftsmen and graziers of Littondale. A barn bears a doorhead dated 1677 with the initials T.F.A., and a cottage one of 1632 with the initials R.L.C. & H.B.

At the far end of the village green stands the Falcon Hotel, once kept by Marmaduke Miller, local wood engraver and watercolourist, whose work adorns the inn's interior. Staying at the inn, one can fish for trout along four and a half miles of river belonging to the inn, or walk up Cowside Beck to study the rare flowers to be found there.

Littondale is blessed with an abundant variety of flora, Dove's Foot, Cranesbill, Herb Robert, Primrose, Cowslip and Ragged Robin abound along with Lily of the Valley in Arncliffe Wood.

Arncliffe to Great Clowder Settlements

Walk up the track by the side of the Falcon Hotel, past the old School House (notice bell) and on to go through gated stile on right. Follow the path up the field to go over wall-stile and on to go over next stile.

Follow path on to go over three wall-stiles and a broken wall on to next wall-stile (turn around and look up to the right to see the crag-top walled settlement site. It is well worth a short detour to view the site — the foundations of homesteads and enclosures are clearly visible). Pass over the stile and on into the amphitheatre-type settlement area.

Great Clowder Settlements

Below Great Clowder at Dewbottoms, in a natural sheltered amphitheatre, is to be found a Bronze Age upland settlement. This consists of a group of fields and huts with thick boulder walls, and isolated huts and small fields are to be found in the limestone area all around. The site has produced fragments of Bronze Age pottery and numerous burial sites have been recorded.

The wide distribution of these Bronze Age sites suggests that there was a fairly large and well organised population at that time, using the area as sheep and cattle pasture, and having a few large farms plus many smaller homesteads with a number of cultivated fields.

By the Late Bronze Age/Early Iron Age (c.1000 B.C.) the climate became much wetter and cooler and settled farmsteads began to appear on the upland Dales landscape. Dewbottoms is a good example of this development. Here five small fields, adjoining one another, are defined by boundary walls of heavy gravel and turf banks. These may have formed the foundations for a palisade of timber posts. Built in and adjoining these banks there are four circular huts and two rectangular ones. The larger of the circular huts may have been the homestead of the head man of the family group.

Among the limestone scars around the settlement are several enclosures which could have served as sheep or cattle pounds in this wide area of upland limestone pasture.

Great Clowder Settlements to Middle House

Follow path on to go over wall-stile and on through the wide valley to go up and over wall-stile. Walk directly on to Middle House.

Middle House

This 17th century farmhouse has been recently restored by workers of the National Trust. To find such a good mullioned frontage in such a wild spot is a rare gem indeed. Notice the doorhead with the large initials H.K. The farm is situated on the monks' route between Malham and Littondale and is one of the highest farmhouses in the Yorkshire Dales.

Middle House appears in early documents and maps as Midlow House, after Mil Low (Middle House Hill), one of the most prominent hills on the Moor. It is possible that the site is of 10th century Norse origin, but in the 16th century it was a grange farm of Fountains Abbey. The farm is first mentioned as early as 1379, and in 1480 John Brown was shepherd there for the Abbot of Fountains, and kept for him 275 wethers and 30 hogs.

In the 18th century the fields below Middle House were used as fairgrounds for the sale of Scottish cattle, sheep and horses. One famous Craven grazier of the 18th century, a Mr Birtwistle is recorded as having "had 20,000 head of cattle on this field in one summer, every Herd enticed from their native soil and ushered into this fragrant pasture, by the pipe of a Highland Orpheus."

In the 17th century the farm was owned by the Knowle family, but the porch, added in the early 18th century is said to bear the initials of Henry King. His pew in Kirkby Malham church has on the door the initials and date H.K. 1721.

To the south of the house stands the small square dovecote, once a welcome source of fresh meat for the household. The barns and shippons that stand nearby are contemporary with the main house.

The Monks' Road

The Monks' Road is an old pack-horse route between upper Malham and Arncliffe, now a well defined and attractive footpath. A pathway north of Middle House leads from the road down below Flask to Darnbrook House, another former possession of Fountains Abbey.

Inside this house is a stone dated 1664 with the initials I.B. M.B. of the Buck family who leased the property for the first time from the grantee of the abbey lands. A house is first mentioned on the site in 1186.

Middle House
to Mastiles Lane Roman Camp

Follow the track to the rear of the farmhouse on and over to go over stile by gate. Walk down the hill to go over fence-stile. Follow farm lane down to go over cattlegrid by small wood (in the Great Close marshy area over to the left have been found many worked flint microliths and two circular features can be made out).

Continue up the trackway (look over to the right to view Malham Tarn and Highfolds Scar) to Street Gate. Pass through the gate on the left and follow Mastiles Lane on, over ford and on up to the Roman Camp site — its centre is marked by the round base of a monastic cross.

Street Gate, Mastiles Lane

The name Street Gate, along with Streets to the west, recall the ancient paved highway of Mastiles Lane. This highway is part of an ancient monastic wag-gon road that ran from Fountains Abbey to its Malham Moor estates and then onward up to their lands in the Lake District. Sections of the lane may owe their origins to the Iron Age, and parts were most certainly in use during the Roman period.

At Street Gate, just before meeting the Tarn House track, and a few yards back from the road on the north side, there stands a prominent boulder that once served as a base stone for a wayside cross, one of three that stand along-side Mastiles Lane.

It was the custom to erect crosses at major points along the monastic roads to stand as landmarks in bad weather, and to mark other trackways leading from the main way.

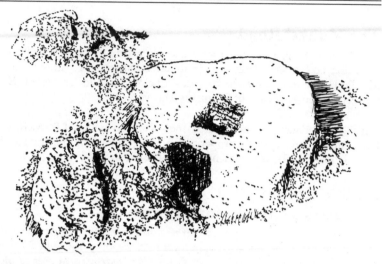

Mastiles Lane Roman Camp

To the east of Street Gate (a significant name), south east of Malham Tarn, is the site of a Roman marching camp that straddles the Lane at a point SD 914655. At the centre of the site is a large round stone with a square socket hole, the base of a monastic roadside cross.

The camp is a rectangular structure marked by a bank and ditch earthwork of about 900ft by 1,000ft, with incurved and protected entries in each side. It would have been constructed by a cohort of Roman soldiers as a temporary stopping point on a route between Ribblesdale and the eastern Dales. During its occupation we can imagine horses tethered on the line, and leather tents laid out in orderly fashion.

Finds of fragments of Roman pottery from the 3rd century and parts of round querns in nearby settlement sites point to a regular contact between the native Brigantes and the Roman forces. The corn that was ground by the querns would have been brought up from the rich growing lands around the Gargrave Villa (Kirk Sink).

Roman Camp to Cote Gill Waterfalls

Follow lane on to walled water tank on left above ford. From here walk back on yourself but heading out onto the moor to pick up pathway. Follow it on to go over wall-stile. Right, and walk up the moor to follow track on up to go through gate and on to go through next gate.

Follow track up to the highest point, then on, heading over to the right to go through wall gate. Follow path on, through gate and on to go down, through gateway (notice lime kiln up on the left) and on down, through gateway and on to above the ravine to view waterfalls.

Cote Gill, Dowkabottom Cave, Arncliffe Cote

To the east of the waterfalls amid a group of ancient enclosures below Hawkswick Clowder is to be found the once inhabited Dowkabottom Cave. The cave was occupied between the 1st to 4th century A.D.

Finds from the site include: pottery, Late 3rd and Early 4th century Roman coins, bronze needles and brooches, bone hair combs and long handled weaving combs, bone buttons, a lead loom weight, an iron arrow head, spindle whorles of Samian ware and perforated teeth of a wolf, used as part of a

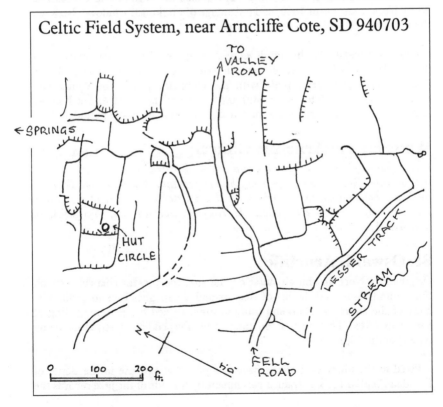

Celtic Field System, near Arncliffe Cote, SD 940703

necklace. It seems like a 'cottage' textile industry was well established in the area during the Roman period. A number of burials were also found in the cave.

Many enclosures surround the cave site with accompanying hut circles, these too belonging to the Iron Age/Romano British period (it should not be assumed that people then actually dwelt in the caves - see Walk 3, the Settle caves on this point).

On our way down to Arncliffe Cote we pass an Iron Age/Romano British field system and associated hut circle (see plan previous page). Notice how the trackways appear to be an integral part of the field system pattern. These fields have survived because they are above the upper limit of mediaeval ploughing.

Below the waterfalls, at Arncliffe Cote, stands the farm of Old Cotes. The house has a datestone of 1650, and a frontage of mullioned windows. Between the porch and the house is a newel staircase turret. All very pleasing.

Lower Littondale was highly developed from the 13th century onwards by the monks of Fountains Abbey into an extensive system of granges. These farms helped to generate trade with the merchant princes of Venice and Florence. Arncliffe Cote was an outlying grange of the larger one at Kilnsey and the track by Cote Gill was established during that monastic period.

Waterfalls to Arncliffe Church

Follow path on, through gateway and on down to enter farm trackway via stile by gate. Follow lane on passing the 17th century Arncliffe Cote Farm to roadway. Follow road to the right to go down first lane on left to footbridge. Pass over stile on left and follow the riverside trackway on, over stiles, to churchyard.

St. Oswald, Arncliffe

Originally a Norman church stood on the site, the present chancel rests on these foundations, and the list of Rectors and Vicars goes back to 1180. The body of the church is plain and uninteresting, ruined by the remodelling of Salvin in 1841. The tower is an interesting Perpendicular structure being typical of the 15th century.

Fixed to the tower wall of the nave is a pike that saw use in the Battle of Flodden Field in 1513. A framed parchment by the side of the pike records the

names of the Littondale men who fought alongside their 'Shepherd Lord', Henry Clifford.

At the Battle of Flodden the English army contingents were organised into 'county groups'. None of the groups was hampered by any clan system as were the Scots. The men from Preston and Manchester had no objection to service with those from Newcastle or York, and the present-day friendly rivalry between regiments had its birth at Flodden.

James IV led an alarmingly heterogenous Scottish army, made up of almost self-contained races: Borderers, Lowlanders, Highlanders and Islanders, each disliking the other. Added to their number were some 5,000 French troops with a large number of Swiss pikes, a new weapon 15 feet long.

Needless to say, the English force won the day, but heavy losses were suffered on both sides. James' body was found on the morning after the battle among a pile of Scottish dead.

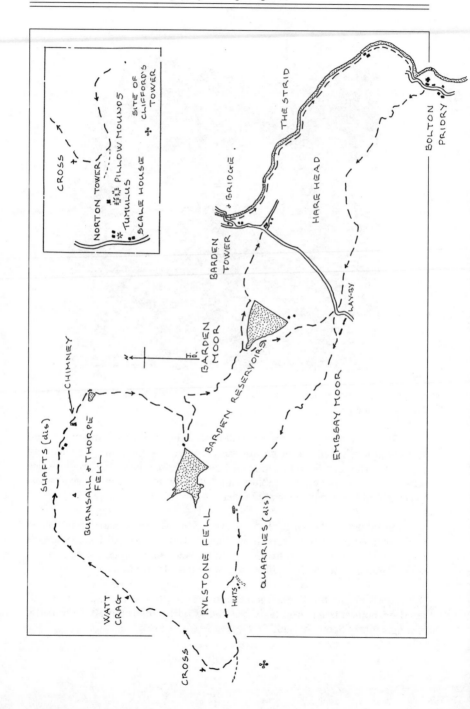

CROSS

NORTON TOWER
PILLOW MOUNDS
TUMULUS
SCALE HOUSE
SITE OF CLIFFORD'S TOWER

THE STRID

BOLTON PRIORY

& BRIDGE

HARE HEAD

BARDEN TOWER

BARDEN MOOR

LAY-BY

BARDEN RESERVOIRS

EMBSAY MOOR

CHIMNEY

SHAFTS (dis)

BURNSALL & THORPE FELL

N

½ml.

RYLSTONE FELL

QUARRIES (dis)

HUTS

WATT CRAG

CROSS

Walk 8

FELL TOWERS AND LOG COFFINS

12½ miles, 7½ miles or full round of 20 miles.

MAP.   *O.S. OUTDOOR LEISURE 10,*
           Yorkshire Dales, Southern Area.

LUNCH: *Take a flask and packed lunch.*
           Tea at Barden Tower Cafe.

START: *Black Hill lay-by, above How Gill, for Barden*
           Moor only.

           Bolton Priory car park for Barden Tower/Strid
           walk, & for full 20 mile round walk.

Viewing the ancient Towers of the Cliffords and Nortons and a few other ancient sites is only a secondary reason for this moorland walk. The major objective is to take in the panoramic views over Airedale and Wharfedale that can be gained from these gritstone heights.

The huge expanse of Barden Moor is a statutory Access Area, so you can freely roam the many trackways subject to by-laws (no dogs, fires or radios, and parts are closed during the late summer grouse shooting season).

The moor bedrock is millstone grit, which, compared to the Craven limestone, is impervious, producing an acidic soil that is the home of heather, bracken and coarse moor grass. Along with grouse rearing, the moor provides grazing for around 2,000 sheep and supplies water to the surrounding villages.

The route described over the moor is a reasonably defined track, following accessways, tracks and bridleways. The section between Bolton Priory and Rylstone is an ancient monastic highway once used by the Augustinian lay brothers. Other tracks lead to old quarry workings, coal and stone were drawn by sledge along these now overgrown hollow-ways.

Bolton Priory

The Priory is described in Volume One, Walk No. 6 in this series.

Some time ago an Anglian socketed spearhead was found in the grounds of Bolton Priory and is now on display in the Craven Museum, Skipton. Notice the fine decoration on the ridge of the head, possibly of c.500.

Bolton Abbey to How Gill Cattle Grid

Walk up the Burnsall road, under the 18th century arch (once an aqueduct) and on to go left onto a track signposted Halton East. (This section of the walk is waymarked with blue signs.) Pass through gate and head across field to footpath sign by side of pond. Follow fence on to go through gate and head over to the right to enter wood.

After a short way take a sharp left-hand turn and continue through the wood to go through wall gate. Follow line of blue stones across two large fields to go through gate. Follow left-hand wall on to skirt Middle Hare Head on the right, over the shoulder of the hill, bearing slightly right, on to go through gate. Follow path on to cattle grid.

The trackway opposite soon joins the higher Black Hill bridleway that leads over the moor to Rylstone, see directions from Black Hill lay-by. If you are on the shorter walk then walk down the road to go left at junction and on to Barden Tower.

Black Hill Lay-by to Rylstone Cross

Follow the moorland bridleway on for some way to go right at junction of tracks and on to go left at next junction and on up and on to signpost. Continue directly on to leave the trackway just before the huts to follow a staked pathway on the right over the moor to reach a wall opening. (The pathway through the opening leads down to Rylstone with Norton Tower on a rise over to the left.) Do not go through the wall opening but follow the wall-side path up to the right, on up to Rylstone Cross via wall-stile.

Norton and Cliffords Towers

In c.1490 John Norton secured the manor of Rylstone when he married the Radcliffe heir female, and so began a series of conflicts that are oft recorded in local history and legend. The popular stories and ballads can be found in the works of other writers, only fact is recorded here.

In the 15th and 16th centuries Rylstone was much more wooded than it is today and harboured many deer within its park. The Rylstone estate bordered onto the hunting lands of the Cliffords of Skipton Castle, overlords of much of Craven, who in their bellicose way hunted freely over the district, including the Rylstone estate, bringing them into conflict with the Nortons.

A letter exists dated 1544 from John Norton which refers to a complaint made by him to Queen Catherine Parr, the King 'being out of the realm', about a Clifford intrusion into the Norton deer park and the adjudication went in John Norton's favour.

John's son Richard as a young man had taken up the family feud and in all probability it was he who built Norton Tower in about 1530. The peel tower, built on the lines of a Norman keep, is sited on the edge of Sun Moor just below the jagged gritstone scarp of Rylstone Fell. Though now a ruin, much of the forty inch thick walls remain.

Higher up on the opposite side of the deep ravine known as Waterfall Gill are the low but visible remains of Cliffords Tower, also called New Hall. This was probably an hunting lodge of the Cliffords, standing as it does on the boundary between the manor of Embsay and Eastby, and that of Stirton and Thorlby.

The Pillow Mounds to the south of Norton Tower I take to be rabbit warrens, similar to those at Friars Head, Winterburn.

Scale House, Oak Coffin Burial

Scale House is a 17th century dwelling, much added to in the Italianate style after 1850. The west front has a porch and two square-topped towers. The south front has a third matching tower to the south-west one.

To the north of Scale House, in the grounds of Scale Hill Farm, can be found a Tumulus around 30ft. in diameter, 5ft. in height and surrounded by a circle of earth at the base. Here an important Bronze Age burial was unearthed by Rev. Canon Greenwell in 1864. The materials of the barrow were soil and flattish stones placed just below the surface over the centre.

In a hollow dug just below the level of the original surface of the ground a rough coffin made of a split tree-trunk was found. The oaken trunk was 7ft. 3ins. in diameter. Within, the inhumed body had so much decayed that the remains were converted into adipocere, but fragments were found of a woollen cloak or shroud in which the body had been enveloped when buried.

The Canon noted that this wrap or cloth extended from head to foot, and thought it probably the ordinary woollen dress of the individual interred in the grave. Bronze implements were also found.

The Cracoe depression is a natural way between south Craven and mid Wharfedale and is marked by important burials at Skipton, Rylstone and Thorpe, and bronze implements at Embsay and Flasby, and by perforated, polished stone axes of early Bronze Age type, at Cracoe and Rylstone.

RYLSTONE CROSS

Rylstone Cross

Rylstone Cross was erected to mark the golden Jubilee of Queen Victoria in 1887. The cross is a modern addition to a mediaeval standing stone set above a dominant gritstone crag, that offers spectacular views over Craven.

Below one can make out the tiny hamlet of Rylstone, once home of the Nortons of whose Hall in the village only the earthworks and fishponds remain. The downfall of the Nortons came with the 'Rising of the North' of 1569 in the cause of Mary, Queen of Scots.

The Norton family, with Richard as its leader, threw themselves into the Rising, perhaps with more ardour since the Cliffords were on the other side. Richard, a member of the Council for the North and holder of other offices, became a front figure in the insurgency and, carrying with him brothers, sons, retainers and tenants, became its literal standard bearer.

For a few months the rebels prospered but they melted away when the Queen's forces (Elizabeth I) were mustered in strength. Richard was attainted for his complicity with his lands going to the Crown and he had to seek refuge in Flanders. One of his sons and one of his brothers suffered death at Tyburn, one son was attainted, another son fled, two sons were tried and later pardoned and two sons took no part in the revolt.

A dozen or so of the common men from the Yorkshire Dales were hanged. Among these was Richard Kitchen, butler to Richard Norton, who was executed at Ripon; another man was hanged at Rylstone and another at Threshfield.

Forty years later the Cliffords gained the Manor of Rylstone as a return for their support for James I.

Rylstone Cross to Cracoe War Memorial

Come back over the stile and follow the wall on, past the R C boundary stone, on up to the War Memorial via stile.

Cracoe War Memorial

This prominent obelisk, a memorial tribute to those in the villages below who gave their all in the Great War, marks the highest point on Cracoe Fell. A stone tablet upon the northern face reads 1914-19, and stones on all faces bear many initials and dates referring to those remembered.

The date of 1919 reminds us that the final Peace Treaty was not signed till that time, and that many West Riding regiments fought till then on the Eastern Front.

Many old hollow-ways can be discerned hereabouts, being the sunken sledge tracks that lead down to the village of Cracoe. It was down these trackways that the stone was brought to build the Cracoe as we see it today. A 1569 survey of Cracoe informs us that most of the buildings in the village were built with crucks of oak, with side walls of turf, stone or wattle, topped with a thatched roof. During the 17th and 18th centuries rebuilding took place in stone with stone slate roof. It was during this period that these old trackways came into being with men climbing each morn to win and hew the rough gritstones on the wild moor.

Apart from fairly modern 18th and 19th century boundary stones one may be lucky to come across certain other more ancient stones. These are marked with the trunk and anlets, being the fess of Clifford, and the annulets of Vipont, dating from c.1580. (Because these stones could be removed by unscrupulous persons you must forgive me for not pointing out their exact location. May the sky fall in on all robbers of our most ancient past, and even of our present. Without a moral code we cannot have a 'society' let alone be a People.)

War Memorial to Old Colliery Chimney

Come back over the stile and follow the wallside path on to pick up a trackway that veers to the right around Burnsall & Thorpe Fell. Follow this shooters trackway on to a house and hut. From the lean-to hut follow the track on to go left at junction down to the old colliery chimney.

Barden Fell Colliery

Up until the turn of the last century, coal was mined from the thin seams on the Moor and used for smelting lead ore on Grassington Moor and also sold for local use. This, like the stone, was transported down from the moor by sledge along the many sunken trackways. Here, in the 'middle of nowhere', we view an old dwelling of some long-gone workman and the ruin and dominant chimney of a former small colliery. Take care not to stray from the pathway, there are many open shafts in the vicinity.

Colliery Chimney to Barden Tower or How Gill Cattle Grid

Follow the trackway down to go right, across sluice of small reservoir and on along the trackway to Upper Barden Reservoir. Follow trackway on down to cattle-grid. A path down to the right crosses the reservoir sluices and works its way on up to How Gill cattle grid.

For Barden Tower follow the main trackway on to the roadway at Barden Scale. Follow the roadway around to the left to Barden Tower.

Barden Tower

The 15th century tower house of the Cliffords is described in Walk 6, Volume 1. Lunches and teas are served on most days from the old Priest's Cottage and Chapel in the Tower grounds. This makes for a good lunch stop in a very romantic setting.

Barden Tower to Bolton Priory, via The Strid

Follow the roadway down to the river and pass over the stile on the east side of Barden Bridge (built in 1659, and repaired in 1676) and follow the path on down through Strid Wood (see Walk 6, Volume 1) to the Cavendish Pavilion and on into the grounds of the Priory.

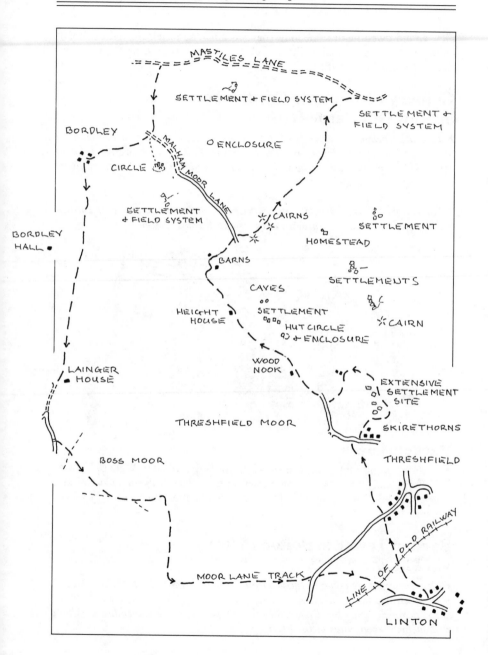

Walk 9

PREHISTORIC SETTLEMENTS

12½ miles.   *Suggest parking your car at Grassington and then walk to Linton via the riverbridge at Linton Falls. A pathway at the bottom left of the National Park car park leads down to the bridge. The roadway then leads you on to Linton Village.*

MAP: *O.S. OUTDOOR LEISURE 10. Yorkshire Dales, Southern Area.*

Take with you a packed lunch and flask.

Country lanes and byways, moorland and limestone, hamlets alive and hamlets now gone, almost every age of the Yorkshire Dales is reflected and brought to light on this truly magnificent ramble.

On the walk we shall get the feel of life on a Iron Age farming settlement in areas that, apart from the lack of trees, are little changed. We also follow the later monastic trackways to their isolated stock farms and hamlets.

Here none of the landscape has changed other than the 18th and early 19th century rebuilding; sheep farming dominates now as it did then.

Linton

Judged by the 'News Chronicle' in 1949 as the North's loveliest village, Linton has lost nothing in that claim. Hidden by mature trees and located only by the use of country lanes it is oft' bypassed by the majority of Dales visitors, and for this we must be thankful.

Those who do visit the village take away the memory of a delightful green surrounded by stone cottages, by a river which is crossed by a clapper bridge, a packhorse bridge and a modern road bridge.

Dominant above the green is the elaborate building of Fountains Hospital believed to have been designed by Vanbrugh. The hospital was built by Richard Fountaine in 1721 to provide then, as it does now, homes for six or seven elderly persons.

On the other side of the green is Linton Hall, a late 17th century building with projecting wing. The porch has a doorway with a semicircular pediment, a cross-window over, and a curvy gable. Across the way the Fountaine Inn provides refreshment in the form of good food and a fine selection of ales.

During the 19th century Linton was a farming and textile centre, with a number of water-powered mills. Wool was brought to the Birkbecks (of Settle) warehouse at Skipton to be sorted and combed then sent out to the Company's mills at Linton and Addingham. Here it was made into stuffs — shalloons, calimancoes, and all sorts of double goods. The three Linton mills provided employment up till the 1860's.

Tourism first discovered Linton after the opening of the Yorkshire Dales railway to Threshfield in 1901. Many of the mill-workers' cottages then going out of use were bought up and improved. Sadly, the railway has gone, replaced by the antisocial private car.

Linton to Threshfield

From the footpath sign by side of road bridge follow track on to go through gate. Walk over to the left to go over old railway bridge and then cross field on a right-diagonal to go through old gateway. Follow wall over on the left on to go through gateway then head down the field to go over wall-stile onto road by houses. Walk up into Threshfield and the Old Hall Inn.

Threshfield

The village stands at a crossroads and on the main route to Wharfedale from Skipton. The majority of its stone houses stand back from the road behind a walled public green complete with the ancient village stocks. In former times the villagers of Threshfield worked a colliery out on the moors to the west.

From the 17th century survives the impressive three-storeyed porch of the manor house. The first floor has a six-light transomed window and the second floor displays a wheelwindow with six spokes and one concentric inner circle. In the gable is a now blocked semicircular window. The Old Hall is dated R.H. 1660, built by the Hammonds.

At Ling Hall lived the Ibbotson family, the famous makers of besoms (a broom made of twigs, like those of witches) which were sold throughout the Dales.

The Grammar school is a fine example of 17th century architecture. Founded in 1674 under the will of the Rev. Matthew Hewitt, it is now a local primary school.

Threshfield to Woodside Settlement

Walk back down the road and over Threshfield Bridge to go through wall-gate on right at footpath sign. Walk directly on to go over stiled foot-bridge on right, then head left across the field to go over wall-stile. Follow left-hand boundary on to go over two wall-stiles, then, on a right diagonal, cross the field to go over wall-stile onto Skirethorns Lane.

Right, and walk on to go up first trackway on the left. Follow track on, right at junction to follow walled trackway on to go through wall-gate. Walk on, veering left, to corner of wall. The extensive settlement area is on the limestone over to the left.

Skirethorns Woodside Settlement

Located at the rear of a large caravan site is an extensive Iron Age/Romano British settlement site. In and among the limestone pavement one can clearly discern the low walls of former buildings and enclosures. In size it is comparable to the Lea Green settlement across the Wharfe and must have been an important centre in its time.

In the Spring months, the floor of the settlement site is carpeted with wild flowers — Orchids, Oxslip, Cowslip, Primrose and Violets compete for the eye. In the nearby woods we find Wood Anemone, Wood Sorrel, Wood Avens and Ramsons.

Woodside Settlement to Cow Close Settlement

Follow wall on into open area and walk directly on to go over wall-stile. Walk down to the left to pass through field gate and walk on by right side of barn to enter caravan site at corner. Follow roadway to the right, right at junction and then left up caravan trackway to go over fence-stile. Follow path on and to the left to go through wall opening and on through next opening above quarry entry. Follow path on to go over corner wall-stile on right before gateway. Follow path down to the left to cross lower roadway to go over fence-stile. Walk down the field to Wood Lane via wall-stile. Walk up the lane to go left up Wood Nook Drive and on past the house to car park. Follow track to the right to go over fence-stile. Cross stream and follow path to the left (yellow markers), over wall and round to the left to go up between rises to go over old wall. The settlement site is on top of the limestone reef knoll.

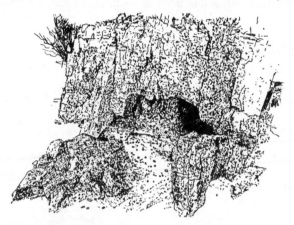

Cow Close Settlement/Cave Scar

Mesolithic (intermediate Stone Age folk) tools have been found in Calf Hole Cave on Cave Scar below the Cow Close hill top settlement. The most important being a chisel-like tool, made by setting part of a

CANINE TOOTH OF BOAR SET IN REINDEER ANTLER + USED AS ADZE

boar's tusk into a reindeer horn handle. These people fished in the glacial tarns left by the retreat of the ice, and would have used the caves for shelter. The cave was first opened in 1890 and yielded bones of bison, reindeer and wolf. Nearby were found an iron spearhead and fragments of earthen vessels.

On the limestone summit above Cow Close we find a typical Brigantian settlement site, a series of rectangular walled dwelling houses, the central domain of a family of herdsmen/women.

Cow Close to Mastiles Lane Summit

Follow path on to go over wall-stile and on to Height House. Pass through gateway and walk directly on following yellow markers (notice caves back over to the left) to go through wall opening and down to barn.

Pass over stile on left at top gate and follow left-hand wall on and up to go over stile and wall-stile opposite. Follow bridleway to the right, through gate and on to Malham Moor Lane via gate. Pass through gate opposite and follow bridleway (waymarked in blue) on, past low burial cairns on summit, down to go through gate and on to enter Mastiles Lane. Follow Mastiles Lane up to the left to the bench-marked stone near the summit.

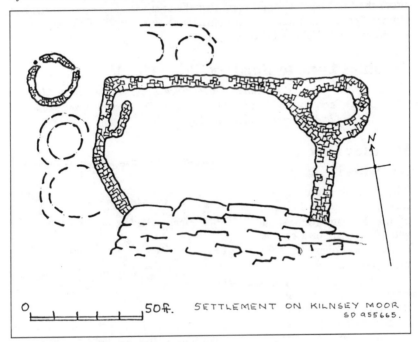

O ————————— 50 ft.   SETTLEMENT ON KILNSEY MOOR
SD 955665.

Mastiles Lane, Kilnsey Moor

Mastiles Lane was a mediaeval monastic trackway, here traversing Malham and Kilnsey Moors. Bases of wayside crosses are still evident along its length. It was used in the late 18th century onwards by lead miners to transport smelted lead to Malham and Settle.

From the bench-marked stone near the summit of the Lane, looking back east and over to the right one can make out the low remains of a small settlement consisting of circular huts and adjoining yards of Romano British type. These sites are scattered all over Upper Wharfedale up to 1,700 ft. and usually have no means of defence.

The domestic items of a typical family include numerous roughly-made bowls and jars and a few imported vessels of samian or colour-coated wares, with stone or lead spindle whorls, bone weaving combs, and perhaps a quern for grinding grain.

On our way down to Mastiles Lane we passed a number of burial cairns. From the finds here it would seem that the area was used as a cemetery in Bronze Age times. A similar cairn-burial area exists on the limestone above Giggleswick (see Volume IV, Settle walk).

Mastiles Lane to Bordley Stone Circle

Follow lane on to Mastiles Gate. Follow track down to the left to Malham Moor Lane. Pass through gateway on left and walk across the brow of the hill on the right to look over the wall at Bordley Circle.

Bordley Circle, SD 949653

The circle lies on Malham Moor, 200 yards due west of the Malham Moor Lane gate. It consists of a circular bank, 50 feet diameter, 3 feet high and about 9 feet wide, originally set with upright stones. Over the years most of the stones have been removed for the making and repair of the adjoining walls. It is known locally as the 'Druid's Altar', as at one side was a trilithon, a large flat stone resting across the top of two standing stones. This was sadly destroyed many years ago.

The site represents a chambered tomb of the round cairn type, a product of the Bronze Age.

Here at Bordley Circle, as at Yarnbury Henge, Pendle is the dominant feature on the skyline, and again it may have played an important role in the siting of this monument.

Bordley Circle to Bordley

Return back to trackway and take the Bordley bridleway to Bordley.

Bordley

Bordley was once a sheep farming settlement of Fountains Abbey and still retains much of the character of a monastic hamlet. Here would dwell herdsmen and shepherds who would help tend the sheep and cattle. The sheep were brought down off the fells to Kilnsey to be clipped, and the wool carried away from there in wains, to the Abbey. Most of what we see today dates from the early 19th century; one house bears the date 1818, with the initials R.M.P.

Bordley to Lainger House

Leave by the Boss Moor bridleway and follow the track on, past the waterfall and on (Cracoe, Rylstone and Flasby Fells come into view) to Lainger House.

Lainger House

What a remarkable find in such an 'end-of-the-road' place, an unusual 17th century dwelling. In the gable of the fascinating two-storeyed porch is a round headed three-light stepped window under a fanciful hood-mould. The oddly detailed lintel bears a date of 1673, and is of a type once popular in the old West Riding.

Lainger House to Linton

Follow lane on and up to go over cattle-grid. From here follow the moorland trackway on the left (notice old quarry workings), across a more well-defined trackway and on over the moor to join another trackway. Follow this new track to the left on down to go left at fork and on to go through gateway and on down to stream. Follow path to the right to go over wall-stile and on down the moor to join lower track above gully. Left, and follow this track on to enter the gated Moor Lane track. Follow this track on to cross main road and follow trackway opposite on and into Linton.

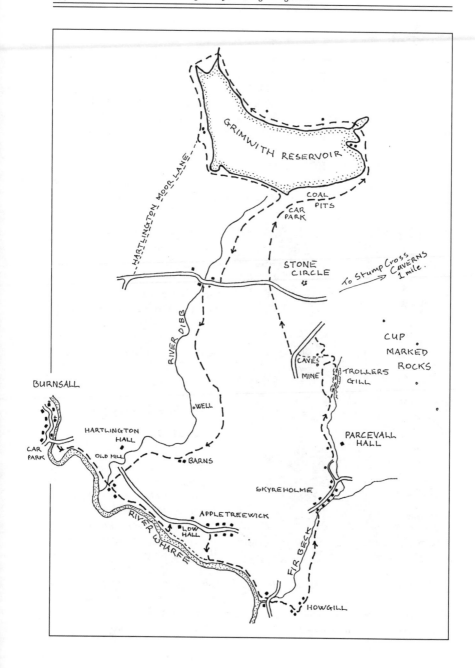

Walk 10

HOME OF THE GRAIL KNIGHT

*6, 9, or 15 miles. Suggest parking at Burnsall for the longer
walks, and by the reservoir for the short walk
and if a lunch stop at Appletreewick is required.*

MAP: *O.S. OUTDOOR LEISURE 10.
Yorkshire Dales, Southern Area.*

LUNCH: *Craven Arms or New Inn, Appletreewick
or Red Lion, Burnsall.*

On this walk we follow the Wharfe from Burnsall, via Appletreewick to Howgill below Simon's Seat. Then wander up onto the moors taking in the limestone gorge of Trollers Gill. After a tour of Grimwith Reservoir we follow the
green valley of the Dibb down to Hartlington and the Wharfe at Burnsall once
again.

The villages, natural features and ancient sites that the ramble takes in are
truly a joy to behold and a pleasure to explore.

For ease of the text we start the walk with a description of Burnsall.

Burnsall

Burnsall is mentioned in
the Norman Survey, 'Brin-
shale', denoting a former
Scandinavian settlement.

BURNSALL CHURCH.

The village is delightfully
situated at a river crossing
alongside a bend of the
Wharfe, framed with trees
and seen against the hilly
background, it is a true

picture indeed. The Red Lion Inn, once the Bridge End Inn caters well for both walkers and tourists, well worth a visit.

On our way through this charming settlement to visit the church we come upon the old Grammar School, an outstanding edifice more like a manor house. It was built in 1605 by Sir William Craven, a wealthy merchant and once Lord Mayor of London. The boys were to be taught English and Latin, with writing and arithmetic added for a small charge. Today it serves as the local primary school. Also while in the village, see if you can locate the four ancient holy wells.

Church of St. Wilfrid

For the most part the building represents the course perpendicular of the 16th century with restorations in the 17th and 19th centuries. Of the 13th century church only portions remain, these being the windows in the south-east corner and two windows which were later removed to the extreme north-east and south-west corners of the church, and the now blocked-up doorway in the north wall.

In the old north chantry is to be found an alabaster altar with reredos panel depicting the Adoration of the Magi dated from the 15th century being Flemish in origin.

The most important features in the church are the twelve pre-Conquest fragments of crosses and gravestones, not forgetting the early Norman font.

The latter is circular on a square base with crude animal decoration around the base of the bowl in a Norse/Danish style.

Nearby are two hog-back tombstones: one, almost whole, with the tiled roof being supported by two muzzled bears; the other, of which only half survives, is a round-topped mass with traces of bears' heads. The Hog-back represents a 'house of the dead' being a memorial stone of the Scandinavians who settled here in the 9th and 10th centuries.

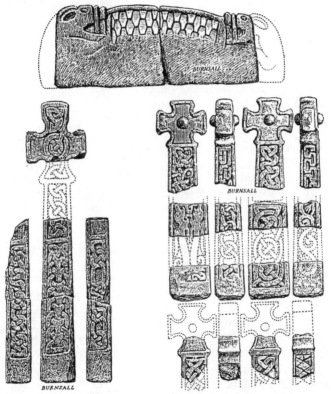

The fragments of Anglo-Norse crosses for the most part belong to the 10th century and are all of the local grit. The workmanship is very careless in both design and cutting and may have been copied by a local workman from others seen elsewhere. One fragment still bears traces of red lead pigment, reminding us that, in their day, these sculptures were gaily painted with reds, yellows, blues and greens.

Two cross-heads are penannular in design, almost approaching a wheel-head and belong to the 11th century. The shaft to one of these cross-heads is limited to only a small patch of ornament on the upper faces. This economy of design places it firmly late in the pre-Norman period.

In pre-Conquest times Burnsall seems to have been a place of some important religious significance, standing as it does on the junctions of ancient north-south, east-west trade routes.

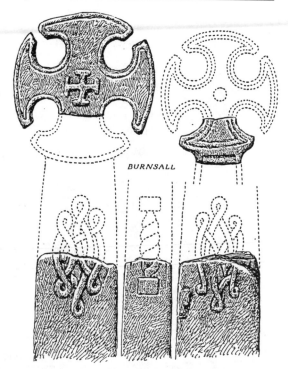

BURNSALL

The dedication to St Wilfrid may owe much to the Romille family (founders c.1150), but the nearby riverside well of St Helena may point to an ancient origin for the site.

Before leaving the churchyard notice the old village stocks in their original position near the Village Hall in line with a row of cottages which once stood here before the churchyard was extended in the 19th century. The lych-gate, with its unusual centre post, is late 17th century and thought to be the only one in Yorkshire, being one of possibly only twelve in the country.

Burnsall to Appletreewick

From the Red Lion, cross Burnsall Bridge to pass through gate on right. Follow "Dales Way" on and up to the left. Following riverside path on, through 17th century Woodhouse Farm and on past barn (once a 17th century house) to follow riverside path on to Appletreewick footpath sign. Follow walled trackway on left to roadway, right and walk up the road, past Low Hall and Craven Arms to the New Inn.

Appletreewick

The little church of St John the Baptist was built out of two cottages in 1898 and improved in 1933. The oak altar rails, reredos, and pulpit are by Clarke of Burnsall, and the pews and other woodwork are by Thompson of Kilburn.

Several houses in the village are worthy of note: High Hall is a 17th century three-storeyed house with a porch formerly of two storeys. Inside, the house retains its original plan with a hall and minstrels' gallery, fine oak panelling and elaborate plasterwork abound, and one window has 720 leaded lights. The house was built by the Craven family whose arms in plaster are above a mantelpiece in the hall.

Low Hall, built by the Preston family, stands at the western approach to the village. The house dates from 1658, but was altered in 1868. Behind the Hall are a number of cottages dating from 1690 which display a wealth of architectural detail — mullioned windows with carved lintels, doorways with masons' marks, oak-pegged doors and stone troughs — all very inviting.

By far the most interesting house is Mockbeggar Hall or Monks Hall, a 17th century rebuilding of a monastic grange of Bolton Priory. The projecting east wing offers a very curious facade (pictured here): the doorway is reached by an outer staircase between which are two windows with lintel-stones decorated with semicircles with pigeon-holes above. A doorhead on the recessed wing bears a date of 1697, and above this is an older stone head of the 'celtic' type.

Although renowned for its sheep fairs, Appletreewick was, for a long time, a centre of lead mining. In 1300 the manor was sold to Bolton Priory, who worked the local mines with vigour through till the later Middle Ages.

The village is also well endowed with two very good inns: the Craven Arms near the village stocks, and New Inn, both renowned for good food and ale.

On our riverside walk to Appletreewick we passed the farmstead of Wood-house. Formerly Woodhouse Manor, it is one of Yorkshire's 'lost villages'. In monastic times it was the property of the priory of Marton-in-Cleveland, and afterwards that of the Clifford's of Skipton, who were followed by yeomen owners. Of the 16th/17th century hamlet only the manor house, now the farmhouse, and one other house, now a barn, remain.

Appletreewick to Parcevall Hall

Pass through the 'toll-gate' (5p) opposite the New Inn and walk down to the river to follow it down (notice 'A'— Appletreewick boundary marker) to Howgill Bridge. Cross bridge and follow trackway on left up to Howgill Lane.

Left, and walk on past Howgill Lodge and Barn (dated 1750, with the initials T. H. S.) to go left at gate (footpath sign).

Follow track on, through gateway and on (Parcevall Hall can now be seen ahead of us in the trees) and across field to go over wall-stile, then walk down to go over footbridge and wall-stile. Walk on to go over stile and follow roadway to the right, passing 17th century Lane House Farm to go left at telephone box and on to the bridge below Parcevall Hall.

Parcevall Hall

After the Dissolution, the manor of Appletreewick passed through many hands, till at length it was purchased by Sir John Yorke of Gouthwaite in Nidderdale; and the younger sons of the family lived at Parcevall Hall. The house, for long in use as a farmhouse, was considerably restored by Sir William Milner in the 1930's and is now a retreat centre for the Diocese of Bradford. The terraced gardens of the Hall are open to the public.

The Hall's name recalls the Grail Knight, Perceval of Arthurian myth, immortalised in Wolfram von Eschenbach's 'Parzival', and later in Wagner's opera 'Parsifal'.

Perceval, or to give him his real name, Peredur, was once the British King of York, killed in 580, one of the last of the great dynasty of Coel Hen who mediaeval fantasy turned into 'Old King Cole'.

Our path from Parcevall Hall to Grimwith leads us by the gorge known as Trollers Gill, set amid an area of rugged limestone. The Gill has its rise on Craven Moor, near the now Dry Gill, below Stump Cross Caverns. It runs its course like the Trolls it is named after — swift and forbidding at one time, gay and sportive at another.

It is curious that all the way down Trollers Gill Trollius Europoeus grows in golden gem-like tufts among the stones and moss, where the water can sprinkle its moisture-loving leaves.

Many stories of boggarts and their wilful ways are told locally about this place, and in an area of old mine shafts and limestone caverns this is only to be expected.

The old mines and caves we pass on the way are dangerous places so keep well away from their inviting and consuming mouths. Keep a good eye on children in such places.

Parcevall Hall to Grimwith (Stone Circle) via Trollers Gill

Pass through gate by side of bridge and follow path on via gates and stiles to the footpath sign pointing up to the left at the mouth of Trollers Gill (there is no definitive right-of-way up Trollers Gill gorge but stiles exist for access through. The path goes around the hillside and enters the gorge via a wall-stile. At the end of the gorge, marked by iron bars set across the stream, a path leads up to the left to go over a stile and on to the public trackway above the old valley mine workings).

Follow the path up to the left to go past the old mine workings and on up the trackway to roadway. Left, and walk on to go over corner wall-stile by gate on right to follow green-lane on, through gate and on to the roadway opposite the reservoir trackway. The Stone Circle is above an old quarry whose entry gate is up the road on the summit of the hill.

Grimwith Stone Circle

The circle stands on high ground (private land) at Farncarl Top. It is made up of seven stones and is c.21ft. in diameter and is similar to the Dumpit Stone Circle some two miles to the west. To the south-east of Farncarl are a number of cup-marked rocks of a type like those to be found on Ilkley and Rombalds Moor.

The lead mines in the area are known to have been worked in Roman times and ore extraction hereabouts is thought to go back to the Bronze Age. The circle may represent a centre of trade for the economic activity of the area. The cup-marked stones remain an enigma.

Grimwith to Burnsall

Follow the Grimwith Reservoir trackway on and around the reservoir to follow the Hartlington Moor Lane trackway back to roadway.

Left, and walk on down to cross Dibble's Bridge and over stile on right. Follow path on up to go over wall-stile and on to go through gateway and over rise to go over wall-stile. Follow path on and over the hillside to pass through gates on left. Right, and walk on to go over stile by sheepfold up to the left. Walk on to follow wall to the right, through gate and then over wall-stile and on, over stiles to still follow wall on to gated trackway. Follow lane down to the right (signed Hartlington), right at barns on down to the roadway.

Walk down the track opposite to Woodhouse to pass over footbridge on right. Follow "Dales Way" back to Burnsall.

*Alternatively one can walk over the dam and walk down the access track to the roadway, then walk down to Dibble's Bridge to go over stile on the left (as you walk down to the bridge notice the boundary stone on the left marked with a cross).

Hartlington

Hartlington, mentioned in the Norman Survey, remains still a tiny hamlet made up of a Hall, an old mill, a former inn and a few scattered houses.

Hartlington Hall dominates the hillside, a fine house that was built by Colonel R. H. Dawson in 1894. During the Second World War it was occupied by the boys of Leeds Grammar School.

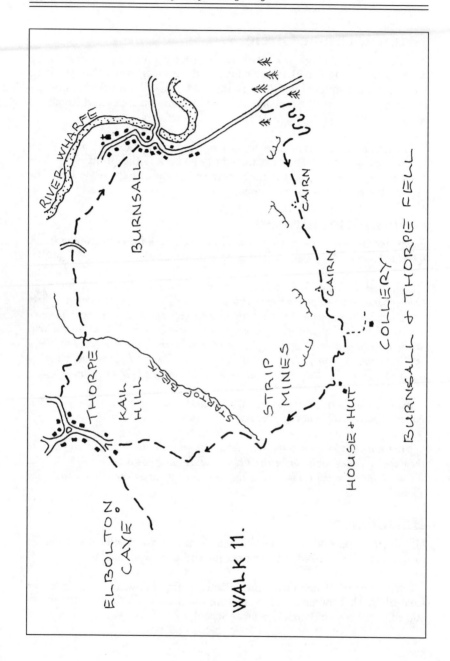

RIVER WHARFE

BURNSALL

THORPE

KAIL HILL

STRIP BECK

STRIP MINES

CAIRN

CAIRN

HOUSE + HUT

COLLERY

ELBOLTON CAVE

BURNSALL + THORPE FELL

WALK 11.

Walk 11

CLOGS, COALS AND CAVES

6 miles.   *Car parking at Burnsall*
              with lunch at Burnsall on return.
MAP: *O.S. OUTDOOR LEISURE 10.*
              Yorkshire Dales, Southern Area.

This short walk allows us a view of and from the summit of Burnsall and Thorpe Fell, a chance to explore an ancient cave burial site and one of the area's most hidden treasures — the hamlet of Thorpe-in-the-Mountain.

Burnsall to Burnsall & Thorpe Fell

Follow the Barden road past the riverside car park and on up to the wood. Take the access trackway on the right and follow it on up through the wood to go over stile onto the moorland fellside. Follow the old sledge tracks that zig-zag up the hillside, past the stone outcrops to the ridge. Follow the ridge over to the right through rough heather for some way to make your way round to a cairn. Here a firm path leads east to join a major trackway. Follow the trackway on to the felltop buildings.

Burnsall & Thorpe Fell

During the 16th and 17th centuries, stone was quarried from these moors and such names as Fairies Chest Quarry and Deer Gallows Quarry are tempting to the mind. The quarried stone was brought down from the moor by drag sledge, and the deep-cut sledge tracks can be seen coming down off all the edges of the moor. In some of the quarries one can still find millstones, stone mullions and sills of 17th century type, and ridge stones for stone-slate roofs.

The buildings around us at the moment are all that is left of an 18th and 19th century coal mining enterprise. The colliery chimney can be seen down the way. The majority of coal was extracted using a strip/drift mining technique the results of which can be seen on the track down to Thorpe. The coal was transported to the lead smelting mills around the Grassington area by way of the deep hollow-ways running down the fell.

Felltop Shelter to Elbolton Cave

From the entrance of the stone shelter just below the house follow the northern track directly in front of you on and down the moor (the ridges running off to the side are old drift-mine workings), past the quarry (notice the remains of a tiny stone building with a hearth — possibly a 'tally-out' station for the coal sledges) and on down to go through gateway.

Follow the lane down to go left before entering Thorpe. Follow this trackway on to the foot of Elbolton reef knoll. Look up to the limestone outcrop, Elbolton Cave lies at its base.

Entry into the cave is via a drop that requires rope and some expertise — consult a caving group if you wish to enter and keep children away from the hole — A FALL WILL BE FATAL.

Elbolton Cave

Elbolton Cave is one of a number of underground systems to be found in this limestone reef knoll. Mine shafts have also been driven into the hillside. When the cave was excavated, sherds of Peterborough Ware, food vessel and collared urn proved occupation during the late Neolithic and earlier part of the Bronze Age. At a later date, burials were made in the cave. Along with the fragments of pottery, the bones of domesticated animals — sheep, cattle, goats, and

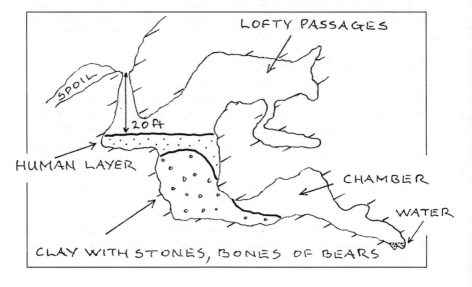

others such as otter and beaver — were found. Some of the bones had been carved into tools, and the canine tooth of a bear had been made into a bone whistle.

Beneath the 'human layer' was a deposit of glacial clay and stones and amongst this was found the bones of Cave Bear. We doubt that people actually lived in the cave and that it was used as a refuge, store, burial site and dump at various times. Their settlement was probably on the site of Thorpe village.

Elbolton to Thorpe

Return to the lane and follow it on into the village.

Thorpe

Upon entering the rustic hamlet of "Thorpe-in-the-hollow", hidden above the valley floor between the two reef knolls of Kail and Elbolton, it is plain to see how it came down in local legend as once being a secret place of refuge for the villagers hereabouts against bands of marauding Scots.

A hundred years ago this now sleepy hollow was a busy place, inhabited by a colony of cobblers who provided the sturdy boots for the lead workers, fell-top coal miners and stone quarrymen of Wharfedale. The place is ageless, it never seems to change; the old ruined houses and barns with fallen roofs and blocked-up windows stand between the plain stone dwellings of country folk, all set around a walled village pound-cum-green.

Some of the buildings are in the Venetian style, displaying the evidence of former wealth. Set in the gable of one of these buildings is a curious stone head.

Thorpe to Burnsall

Walk up the eastern lane to bend then follow walled trackway on and down to go over wall-stile. Follow path down, through gate and on down to the left to pass through wall-gate. Cross stream and follow path up to go through wall-gate and on to go through next wall-gate.

Walk across the field to drop down to gateway (footpath sign) to follow wall on to cross lane via wall-stiles. Walk on over the rise to go over wall-stile, then walk down to the right and on to go over a number of wall-stiles to Burnsall via cottage yard.

OTHER WALKING BOOKS
BY JOHN DIXON

'HISTORIC WALKS IN THE RIBBLE VALLEY'
1987. Dalesman.

'HISTORIC WALKS AROUND PENDLE'
1988. Dalesman.

'HISTORIC WALKS AROUND BLEASDALE
1988. Carnegie Press.

'HISTORIC WALKS AROUND RIBCHESTER'
1988. Carnegie Press.

'HISTORIC WALKS AROUND THE WEST PENNINE MOORS'
1988. Carnegie Press.

'HISTORIC WALKS AROUND THE FOREST OF BOWLAND'
1989. Carnegie Press.

'HISTORIC WALKS FROM THE LEEDS & LIVERPOOL CANAL'
1990. Carnegie Press.

'HISTORIC WALKS AROUND THE PENDLE WAY'
1990. Aussteiger Publications.

'WALK & DISCOVER THE RIBBLE VALLEY'
1990. Ribble Valley Borough.

'WALK & DISCOVER WHALLEY VILLAGE
1990. Ribble Valley Borough.